THE

COURAGE

TO

CONTINUE

THE

COURAGE

TO

CONTINUE

A FAMILY'S LEGACY OF RESILIENCE
AND GLOBAL ENTERPRISE

Advantage | Books

ITZHAK FISHER

Published by Advantage Books, Charleston, South Carolina.
An imprint of Advantage Media.

ADVANTAGE is a registered trademark, and the Advantage colophon is a trademark of Advantage Media Group, Inc.

Printed in the United States of America.

10 9 8 7 6 5 4 3 2 1

ISBN: 979-8-89188-234-8 (Paperback)
ISBN: 979-8-89188-235-5 (eBook)

Library of Congress Control Number: 2025901368

Cover design by Matthew Morse.
Layout design by Ruthie Wood.

This publication is designed to provide accurate and authoritative information in regard to the subject matter covered. It is sold with the understanding that the publisher is not engaged in rendering legal, accounting, or other professional services. If legal advice or other expert assistance is required, the services of a competent professional person should be sought.

Advantage Books is an imprint of Advantage Media Group. Advantage Media helps busy entrepreneurs, CEOs, and leaders write and publish a book to grow their business and become the authority in their field. Advantage authors comprise an exclusive community of industry professionals, idea-makers, and thought leaders. For more information go to **advantagemedia.com**.

03-06-2025 4:19

CONTENTS

✳

AUTHOR'S NOTE

A handful of years ago, my wife, Ruthie, and I had our portrait painted by one of Israel's most prominent artists. That encounter took place because many years prior, Ruthie got me interested in collecting art—paintings in particular. She was the one who bought the first two paintings we ever owned. And she bought them for a very practical reason: we had empty walls in our apartment. In one sense, I suppose, that's a nice problem to have in Manhattan.

We acquired those first two paintings the same way we got the apartment: Ruthie did all the legwork. When it came to those paintings—and guided by her mother's steady advice, "If it's nice, you buy it"—she got in contact with a couple of art consultants … and that's how our collection got underway. Ruthie even bought a Soyer that first day without yet knowing how famous he was. She has a good eye.

Abstracts, landscapes … they mostly don't do it for me. I'm drawn to faces. I like to be surrounded by people. Every person has a story, and I like to learn what I can about that story.

There's a painting by Lennart Anderson in our apartment—a woman's face. When I bought it from the artist, he said to me, "My wife told me that I will never sell this painting." When I asked why, he answered, "This is the portrait of a student of mine who fascinated me." We have another very moving painting by Mary Beth McKenzie, which I learned was the first painting she created after being diagnosed with multiple sclerosis. Knowing that changed something about what I see when I look at it.

From these paintings and others, I've come to believe that the connectedness between painter and subject is almost never random. I may not personally know the people whose portraits hang in our apartment, but I know something about the relation of the artists to those people. This is important to me when I'm buying a piece—I don't just want to feel connected to a work; I also want to understand something about its making. I want the story behind the story. To get that information, I often have to dive a layer below what most people might be able to find out from consultants, dealers, catalogues—sometimes even from the artists themselves.

For a time, I researched portraits painted by Israeli artists, whom I generally wanted to support. It helped, too, that our good friends in San Diego, Jeff and Vivien, were—and are—big art collectors. They introduced us to a number of artists, several of whom we adored.

My research ultimately connected me to a consultant from Israel with a tremendous eye for artists who are going somewhere. It was that consultant who introduced me to Aram Gershuni, one of the best portrait artists in Israel and the man who painted the portrait of Ruthie and me. I wanted to understand the process of portrait painting and thought seeing firsthand how he worked might offer some unique insights, so we decided the two of us would sit for a portrait.

Seven days a week, for six weeks, I sat for three hours, and then Ruthie sat for three hours. I took a picture of the work in progress after every session, two pictures a day, to track the whole thing as it came into being.

Having our portrait painted was a valuable experience for Ruthie and me. We watched as little transformations occurred on a daily basis. The painting itself changed at least thirty or forty times—even our expressions morphed along the way. Though it was overall a very time-consuming process, Ruthie and I were both blown away by the speed at which certain shifts took place, including the artist's ability to add in, with great skill, a little detail like a necklace or an earring.

I think the whole thing was a valuable experience for the artist, too. Ruthie gave him a free three-hour-long therapy session every day for six weeks. I think the story behind our portrait is that Ruthie learned a lot about the painter.

Then, at the end of the process, all three of us—Ruthie, the artist himself, and I—were horrified. Having taken pictures of his progress every day, I can say that it was never obvious at any point along the way that the final portrait was going to be terrible.

Reflecting on it now, I think about how he didn't really know our personalities very well before painting us—that I like to laugh, for example. When the completed painting arrived, I told him that Ruthie and I both looked like we had just received some very bad news. He took me to the portrait room at the Metropolitan Museum of Art, stood with me in the middle of the room, and said, "Show me one portrait of somebody smiling."

I looked all around me and then said, "You know what? They all look depressed, too."

But for me it was more than that—more than just the jarring experience of being memorialized not looking happy or content. In the portrait, I look as if I've had a lot of Botox. My laugh lines, for example, are completely absent. I see them every day on my face, but they're nowhere to be found in that painting. The rendering of Ruthie's face is not so bad. She's a bit more accurately presented, and maybe that's because Gershuni got to know her better during their daily sessions.

In the end, Ruthie was happy because she looks pretty good; I still look like a Botox guy. We hung the painting at the entrance to our bedroom, where no one except us has to see it. We've occasionally shown it to friends, and some of them have suggested that it's similar in style to *American Gothic*, the famous Grant Wood piece.

What I find spot on about that comparison—funny, even—is that *American Gothic* is a painting that was the subject of some debate: Is it a caricature of people out of step with the modern world or an homage to humble beginnings and strong, lasting values?

Though you might not expect it, that question brings me straight to the matter of this book and its contents. Ruthie, I need to tell you, was and remains absolutely opposed to my idea that we should write our story.

I think about writing this book as an opportunity to talk about our parents, the influence of our upbringings on our lives, the strange and lucky and often wonderful experiences we've had, and our hopes for our children and their children. We are links in the chain of our families' complicated histories. One hundred years from now, if one of our great-great-grandkids decides to pull this book off the shelf, I imagine them saying, "Wow, Itzhak and Ruth had some amazing experiences, and they had a fantastic sense of humor about their lives!"

For Ruthie, there's something about writing about ourselves that she finds deeply unnerving. It's one thing that my curiosity required her to sit for a portrait that hangs on our bedroom wall. It's wholly another thing to try putting our experience into words—words that might be printed and shared with ... who knows? She's worried that we'll end up in these pages as caricatures of ourselves, some of our qualities and features exaggerated, others entirely left out.

As someone who looks every day at a portrait of himself without his laugh lines—in my opinion, one of my defining facial features, representative of one of my defining personality traits—I can't say that I'm so bothered by that possibility. Do I want us to create a truthful account of our lives, one that reveals our hearts? Of course I do. Am I so worried that we'll end up the *American Gothic* version of ourselves in book form? No. By that I mean we may, in these pages, end up with a written version of ourselves that puts too much emphasis on some life events and not enough on others. Heck, by the time Ruthie is done redacting parts of my stories and tempering some of my "tell it like it is" insights, we may end up looking a bit odd. Still, I hope we'll seem enough like ourselves for the generations to come to believe that we did a pretty good job finding ways to support our family and be content with this life.

For now, let me say this: If you find yourself reading this book, you might just be related to us. Or, if Ruthie decides that it's okay for us to print more than one copy to keep on our bedroom bookshelf, maybe you'll connect with our story, even if you don't know us directly.

CHAPTER 1

The weather forecast projected rain, but it turned out to be a beautiful sunny day. Ruthie and I were participating in the Rwandan government's eighteenth annual national celebration of the country's efforts to preserve and conserve nature. The premiere event, Kwita Izina, is a big ceremony where the mountain gorilla infants born in the past year are given special names to recognize their great value to the nation. The ceremony for the gorillas is based on a traditional Rwandan ceremony for naming human infants shortly after they are born. But the mountain gorillas are named after qualities, ideals, and values, like Charity or Harmony or Destiny. People come from all over the world to witness them receiving their names.

Right now, I'm the chairman of the Rwanda Development Board, which has, among other things, charge over preserving the gorillas, the mountain, and all the tourism associated with them. That said, I'd never had the opportunity to be part of the gorilla naming until this day. I travel to the country four times a year helping to bring in productive business investments; Ruthie usually accompanies me on one of those visits each year. Given that Ruthie and I were part of the group naming the twenty or so new gorillas in September 2022, we timed her annual visit to coincide with the ceremony. We also brought American rabbi David Wolpe, our friend and pollster Frank Luntz, and good friends from New York Eti and Yair, Limi and Neri, and Jennifer and Mark.

The way the ceremony usually works—and since this was our first time participating, what we did not know ahead of time—is that the government prepares both the names and the short speeches explaining their symbolic significance. To the contrary, Ruthie and I were working under the assumption that we could choose the name for "our" gorilla. And we'd already come up with a plan. We would name the baby gorilla after Ruthie's father, Leo. Our reason? Well, it was a bit irreverent. We figured that if there is an awakening of the dead, the two of us naming a baby gorilla after Leo would be sure to get him up and moving.

Back in the mid-1990s, I attended the funeral of the Chabad Rabbi, who is called the messiah by the people who believe his existence marked the end of Jewish exile. Everybody was screaming, "Wake up, wake up!" because, in their view, he was not supposed to die. He's been dead all the while since, but to this very day, there is a tent next to his grave where people gather around the clock. If he wakes up, they are going to be there for him. I'm not sure what they intend to do when he arises. Maybe take him home and get him cleaned up and fed. By contrast, Ruthie and I didn't expect that Leo would awaken without some prompting. And we certainly didn't have any plans for what to do with him after witnessing his confusion at discovering himself in Rwanda.

The other thing that I did—again, not knowing how the ceremony works—was ask a Rwandan fashion designer to make us both special outfits. It turned out that everyone was required to wear the same outfit—the men in one design, the women in another—all the exact same color and style. In the end, Ruthie and Limi were allowed to wear their specially made outfits, but all of us men were required to wear identical clothes.

Entering the space set up for the ceremony was a little bit overwhelming. Neither Ruthie nor I expected that there would be so many people—fully forty-five thousand—in such a beautiful setup at the base of Volcanoes National Park. There was a lot of participation from the local villages, which are set up to receive 10 percent of the income from gorilla-based tourism. Back in the day, poachers hunted the gorillas, but keeping them alive has become far more profitable. In response to gorilla-based tourism, the surrounding villages have developed community centers, art galleries, and many other ways of inviting interest and bringing economic development to the area. I don't think I'm being partial when I say that there's a richer experience to be had visiting gorillas in Rwanda than in any of its neighboring countries. There are beautiful lodges around the mountain; you get the experience of being in nature right next to the volcanoes, and a gorilla research center is set up where visitors can spend time learning about the animals and the other wildlife.

I decided to run our chosen name and the words I wanted to speak by the people in charge of the ceremony. They made some edits to my speech and then gave me permission to go off script.

When it was time for the naming, Ruthie and I stepped up to the microphone together. I leaned forward and began.

"The baby we will be naming is a male born on the first of August, 2022. We are naming him Intare, the Kinyarwandan word for lion, after my father-in-law, who was called Leo, which also means lion. Leo was born in a small town in Poland prior to World War II. The Germans sent him to a labor camp and death camp. All forty-five members of the family were exterminated with the exception of Leo, his brother, and one uncle. For Leo, his biggest sources of pride were surviving genocide, having a family in America, and having future generations carry on his people's legacy.

"The most amazing thing about him was his constant smile and his optimism. And that is what struck my wife and me in Rwanda, as soon as we came down the steps of the plane on our first visit here. This place has risen from the ashes and is full of pride and forward-thinking people. It is exciting and vibrant and filled with both the young and old, all working to make it a miracle country. We have a special bond emerging from genocide to redemption."

When we met people afterward, they told us how moved they were by the speech. Our musings about the name for our gorilla had started as an inside joke about the awakening of the dead, but we turned it into something fitting to the occasion in its shared meaningfulness.

I believe Rwanda is a miracle country in many ways. But what stands out to me is the country's decision, after the genocide of 1994, to seek reconciliation with rather than revenge upon that part of the population responsible for mass murder. Myself—I'm not sure that if I were in that situation, I would be able to forgive and live side by side with people who had murdered my family. But when I asked President Kagame, "How do you forgive the people who killed your parents, your sisters and brothers, your neighbors and friends?" he answered, "By living *with* them, we help the country move forward. We didn't have a choice. We had to move forward and try to be a nation."

After the genocide, a million and a half people were in jail. By this fact alone, you cannot have a functioning country. The first ten years afterward, Rwanda remained in shock. But for the past fifteen or so years, the reconciliation system has been successful. The leaders of the genocide were punished, and others who participated had to stand in front of the whole community, including the families whose members they killed, and admit to the crimes they committed. Then, they were put to work rebuilding what they had helped destroy—everything from roads to houses to schools. No one speaks of their tribal lineage any longer. Instead, they are all Rwandans.

As I see it, the most important factor in their ability to live together is the country's economic situation. It's a much different place now than it's ever been. The GDP is growing between 6 and 8 percent a year. Foreign investments are pouring in. Infrastructure is expanding, and access to electricity alone—which in 2008 was at only 6 percent—is at 75 percent today. The country is flourishing. The citizens see that the country is doing well, that the economic situation is better than it was years ago. Those are the circumstances that make it possible to move forward together as one nation.

To me, Rwanda is quite like Israel. Both are small countries surrounded by hostile neighbors, and both have strong armies. The Rwandan army even acquires some of its training and equipment from Israel. One of the big reasons I do what I do for Rwanda is that it is a big friend of Israel on a continent where Israel does not have a lot of friends to begin with. I wouldn't persist in trying to help if Rwanda were an enemy state. And the president's message is not unlike those I grew up hearing in Israel: We can rely only on ourselves. And no one should dare start anything with us, because we will be ready for them.

People ask me, "Why don't you help the Democratic Republic of the Congo?" I have a lot of explanations to offer, but the two I usually focus on are these: Congo has 95 million people compared to 13.5 million in Rwanda. I sense that I can personally make a more significant difference in a smaller country. I also explain that the level of corruption in the Democratic Republic of the Congo is shocking to me. Corruption is so ingrained that it's assumed; it's at the very surface of every deal and transaction. Things are different in Rwanda.

A lot of people there come to me for help, and I am very clear that I do not wish to get paid for whatever assistance I can offer. That's not how I work, and I sense that my approach is respected. Rwandans have clear, public steps for addressing whatever corruption attempts to thrive there. Both the government and the media have processes for flushing out people who are corrupt.

Honestly, those are just a couple of the many reasons Ruthie and I have such affection for the place. That, and when we visited there for the first time just a handful of years ago, on a safari with our friends Vivien and Jeff that took us to multiple countries in the region, Ruthie could not get over how beautiful, clean, and orderly it was. "You should do something here," she said to me on our late-night taxi ride from the airport to our hotel.

Ruthie says I always run with her suggestions like a full-force maniac. Maybe that's true. But she has come to appreciate the products of my enthusiasm. Now, when Ruthie comes to Rwanda with me for her annual trip, the president always hosts a little celebration, and the two of them discuss their families and kids like the best of friends. When the visit ends, Ruthie insists on walking backward out of the room, reminding the president that she refuses to show him any disrespect.

Me, I show President Kagame my respect in other ways. I think it's amazing that one person can change twelve million people's lives as he has. He's doing well by his people. And that country is carrying more than its weight. After COVID-19 precautions were lessened, Rwanda held a summit for thirty-five heads of state—the Common-wealth Heads of Government Meeting—coordinating thousands of participants, lectures, and meals. President Kagame is also now the president of the Commonwealth—a voluntary association in which the member governments agree to work toward shared goals like development, democracy, and peace. And just this past March, the FIFA Congress—with over six thousand people—took place in the capital of Kigali. I find impressive the country's capacity to success- fully host such big events and play a leading role in the region.

There's more to say about my experiences in Rwanda, the way they feel to me like a culmination of all the skills and talents I've developed over a lifetime. But we'll get to that.

For now, I imagine the important thing to know is that Leo did not wake up after becoming the namesake of a baby gorilla. At least … he has not yet.

CHAPTER 2

When we look at the lives our parents created for their children, both Ruthie and I find it amazing that, as survivors of unspeakable trauma, they were able to lead so-called normal lives. They did their very best to offer us some perspective on life and to share with us the positive values that had given shape to—and been shaped by—their own upbringing.

Though Ruthie and I were both very close with our parents, there is not a lot of detail to share when it comes to recounting what we know of their experiences during World War II. We are poor in stories about that time because we barely heard them told. And if we did discover the thread of a story here or there, it was often told bereft of color or emotional resonance. My parents almost never spoke of their experiences. Ruthie's father spoke of his with some regularity but in coded language to his brother and brother-in-law and others, well after Ruthie had been tucked into bed. She remembers lying in bed, awake, listening to family and friends who had gathered in the kitchen as they sat around drinking tea, eating cheese danish and cookies, and talking until late at night. She could barely hear their conversations but was always trying to piece together what she could.

Most of what she overheard involved the group trying to account for what had happened to all the people with whom they had grown up, trying to find those still lost to them.

You already know a little bit about Leo, but I need to introduce you to him once again, to his wife, Celia, and to my parents, Martin and Haviva, in order to give you a sense of the extraordinary odds they'd all faced.

This is what Ruthie and I know of their experiences.

Leo

Ruthie's father was born in a small town in southern Poland—and about an hour and a half north of Krakow—called Kielce. On a visit there midway through our lives, Ruthie decided that the whole town was a dump, but I rather liked the place. Leo and his siblings—a brother and sister—were all raised in a religious home; at that time, there were very few Jewish homes that were not religious. At one point in their youth, the siblings' father went bankrupt. If you were Jewish in Poland in those days, there were very few options for making a living, and both sons understood that it was their responsibility to help the family as they were able.

Ruthie's uncle Shulim was an amateur boxing champion in the region. Though he was quite short, about five foot four, he had unbelievable physical strength, which—we can attest—he maintained throughout the entirety of his life. As a kid, if Shulim heard someone say a negative word about his family, he would turn on his heel and beat them up. He was also something of a rebel—always in trouble, uninterested in practicing the family's traditions, and always sneaking out the windows of their home, climbing down the trees, and heading out toward his next adventure. It wouldn't be unfair to describe him as having, overall, a serious dislike of authority.

Ruthie's father, Leo—if you stretched him—might have been about five foot seven, and his physical prowess was not at all like his brother's.

The Nazis invaded Poland in 1939. Ruthie's grandfather, grandmother, and the three children were sent to the ghetto and then on to Auschwitz. In the death camp, both of Leo's parents, his sister, and his sister's husband perished. The Germans knew that Ruthie's uncle was a prized fighter, so they would put up fights between him and another of the prisoners or sometimes even pit him against one of the guards. Because her uncle fought well and the Germans were suitably entertained, they occasionally gave him additional scraps of food. Shulim shared those extra morsels with Leo, and together the brothers survived the death camps long enough to be moved along to a labor camp. There, they were sent out into nearby fields to risk their lives locating and digging up all the bombs that had not exploded on contact.

The brothers survived that, too, and at the end of the war, they were among those liberated by the Americans. As they walked away from the camp with nothing but the tattered clothes on their backs, the pair eventually came across an abandoned mail train. The brothers decided that the trains were destined for the German troops on the front lines and that there must be cigarettes somewhere inside all the envelopes. Once they finished opening every envelope, they had amassed hundreds of cigarettes.

Leo and Shulim started dealing on the black market, eventually found their way to where all the displaced persons were in Germany, and sold everything you could imagine, from cigarettes to carpets to cameras, from chocolates to currency. With his profits, Leo bought himself nice suits, got himself a driver's license, and purchased the first civilian Mercedes right off the assembly line. Later in life, Ruthie asked him, "What were you trying to do by being the first to own that car?"

"I was trying to make myself into a real human being," he answered.

Immediately postwar, many Jews lived in Germany, but very few of them stayed long term. Within a handful of years dealing on the black market, Leo made the decision to move to America. He wired himself $100,000 (an absolute fortune at the time) and boarded a boat to New York. Ruthie remembers that her parents ultimately had only one or two acquaintances who remained in Germany. Her mother would always remark, "How could anybody stay in Germany and build their life, do business, send their kids to school?" She couldn't imagine her fellow Jews having to look at, let alone live and interact with, the very people who had been their oppressors only a short time before.

Shulim took over the brothers' business in Germany when Leo left. By then he was married to a woman named Luba and had a son. Within a few months, he ran into some trouble and was sent to jail. Though he was jailed for less than a year, his transgression created an obstacle to joining Leo in America. When Shulim's immigration pass to that country was rescinded, he and Luba chose to go to Argentina, imagining it as a waystation on their journey to the US.

Shulim and Luba would call Argentina home for another thirty-five years before finally moving to America. As Ruthie tells it, every phone conversation she ever witnessed between her father and her uncle consisted of her father screaming into the receiver, "You need to get on a plane and move to America!" or "Stop lending other people money and get out of Argentina!"

Every year, Shulim, Luba, and their children would visit New York—Luba even spent whole summers in the city visiting both her sister and Ruthie's family. On one of those visits, Shulim smuggled diamonds into the US from Buenos Aires and was very happy with himself for having successfully transported them in the double bottom of his luggage. When Leo asked to see the diamonds, Shulim took him into another room where he'd left his travel case. He opened the luggage to find it full of women's clothing. Leo ran straight to the bathroom, as was his habit whenever he was stressed, but the other relatives there had the good sense to take Shulim and the mistaken piece of luggage back to the airport. To everyone's surprise, when they arrived, there was Shulim's lone case circling the baggage claim belt.

Though Shulim and Luba visited New York regularly, Leo's visits to Argentina fell off relatively early after one occasion when, during a flight there, a technical difficulty forced the crew to land the plane in the Brazilian Amazon. The crew and passengers waited a full four days for the part they needed so that the plane could once again take flight. For four whole days, Leo believed that his life was over. He refused to travel to Argentina ever again.

Leo didn't work during his first five years in New York. He needed to find himself, as the saying goes, and he could more than afford to do so. When he decided to end his hiatus and find a profession, he learned relatively quickly that he didn't want to work for anyone. He worked one day selling women's clothing in a dry goods store, and at the end of that day he quit, saying to the shop owner, "Mr. Goldstein, you don't have to pay me. I just need to leave." After deciding to be independent, Leo found and financed a business partner, and the pair became a highly successful duo in the optical goods industry. They were importers of eyeglass frames but named their business Exporti- mar—a fact that has always made us laugh. Over the course of forty years, Leo sold millions of frames. His most successful ones early on were a hexagonal metal pair, another style called the General, and a third called the Pilot. The Pilot, which we now refer to as the aviator frame, was introduced to America by Ruthie's father in the 1960s.

When Leo started his business, he was one of only five main importers selling frames to opticians and optometrists. He made it big, especially because it wasn't until the 1970s that big designer houses started getting into the eyeglass business, putting their names and later their logos on frames and then selling them at truly exorbitant costs. Ruthie remembers sitting in the kitchen with her friends helping her father come up with a brand name for Exportimar's frames. Ruthie and her friends suggested Henri de Paris, a style that did well for quite some time against its established luxury-brand competitors.

Celia

Ruthie's mother was born in Krakow, a big city compared to the small one from which Leo hailed. Celia grew up in the company of two siblings—a sister and a brother—and her parents.

When I schlepped Ruthie kicking and screaming back to Poland, we visited the building where her mother had spent her youth. Unfortunately, we weren't allowed into the building—not even the lobby. When the building superintendent came to understand that we were Jews visiting a building in which a family member had once lived, he started screaming his head off. Apparently, he believed we were there to reclaim the apartment despite the fact that it had always been a rental property. He refused to understand when we tried to explain that all we truly wanted was to see, to stand inside, the space where Ruthie's family had lived. Later, we learned from our young tour guide that the superintendent's venomous resistance to our attempt merely to trace our roots is so typical of building managers that it's almost an everyday occurrence.

When war broke out, Celia's entire family was among the Jews put in the ghetto called Plashov. Later they were transported to Auschwitz—the death camp.

Celia's father died at Auschwitz. Her brother survived the death and labor camps, only to be killed just a few days before the liberation. Miraculously, her grandmother, mother, and aunt survived both Auschwitz and the labor camps.

It took Ruthie's mother fifty years before she told us the story of how that happened.

The family had already lived several years in a ghetto before being sent to the death camp. After arriving at the camp, the prisoners were divided into two groups—those selected for work and those selected for extermination. Ruthie's aunt Hela was selected for work. Ruthie's grandmother, already forty-two years old, was selected for the gas chamber. Celia—who was about fourteen years old at the time—saw her mother crying after the selection and thought to herself, *I've had enough. I'll go with her. We'll go together.*

Hela saw what was happening and turned to a nearby officer whom she recognized, begging him to help her. With his assistance, Hela pushed both Celia and their mother from the line. The area where they happened to be standing in line was under construction, so Hela pulled aside a piece of the construction material and helped her mother and sister hide behind it.

The chances of that action being successful were already extraordinarily slim, and slimmer still were the chances that no one would discover them and either shoot them on the spot or put all three of them in the line to the gas chamber.

What happened, instead, was that the officer let the women sleep in the work barracks and the next day assigned them to another camp to work.

After I heard Celia tell this nearly unbelievable story, Ruthie turned to me and said, "I've never asked too many questions. It hurts my mother to talk about it."

We left it at that.

When the sisters and their mother were released from the labor camp by the Americans, Celia and Hela found work at the Joint HIAS in its Frankfurt headquarters. HIAS, or the Hebrew Immigrant Aid Society, is the world's oldest refugee agency, originally established by Jews to help fellow Jews fleeing pogroms in Russia and Eastern Europe. For nearly seven years, the sisters helped relocate World War II refugees. They went to work every day; they bought themselves nice clothes; and they learned English, which gave them a substantial advantage over other survivors who would eventually have to build new lives in foreign countries.

Ruthie's aunt Hela, whose job it was to make official decisions about where each refugee would go, would meet those people years later and remember each of them. "Oh, you! I sent you to Georgia," she'd say in recognition, or "You, I sent you to California ..."

The way the immigration process worked was that a city or town would agree to take in a designated number of refugees but then insist they possess skills applicable to specific professions—so, for example, Atlanta might need tailors or bakers or some other category of professionals to fill a gap in its workforce. Hela would dutifully fill out the official paperwork with "tailor," "baker," and so on to ensure that all the mostly unskilled teenagers she was relocating would be welcomed in some new place and offered another chance at living.

When nearly every refugee who came through the Frankfurt office had been assigned and transported, the program began the process of shutting its doors. The sisters were not sure they wanted to move to the US yet, but one of the HIAS staff warned them: "If you do not take this last plane, you will *not* be going to America." That's how Ruthie's mother, aunt, grandmother, and a cousin finally left Frankfurt in 1952, the very night before the Frankfurt HIAS was shuttered. The borough of Manhattan had closed to immigrants just before the group left Germany, so they were formally assigned to Jersey City instead. When they arrived at the airport in New York, Celia and Hela told their mother, "We are not going to Jersey City. Forget about Jersey City." To them, a metropolitan-area suburb would not suffice.

The sisters convinced HIAS to book them a hotel room in the city, and the next day they went out in search of work and more permanent housing. Hela found work as a bookkeeper; Celia got a job as an office assistant. But Celia did not much enjoy transcribing tape-recorded dictations for her boss. After typing out a whole document in which she mistook the word "abreast" for "a breast," she decided she'd find something less stressful to do. Bookkeeping would turn out to be a far easier task for her.

Leo and Celia met in New York on a blind date arranged through a mutual friend; he took her to a movie and a very nice restaurant. In those days, a young woman's entire family might accompany her on all her courtship activities. In our family, we joke that every time Celia met up with Leo, she brought along anyone she knew who was hungry and needed a free meal. Every time the check came, the relatives headed to the bathroom, and Leo covered the bill.

Within a few months of dating, the couple married. When they arrived at their honeymoon location in Florida, Celia, who was otherwise quite frugal, quickly informed Leo that she forgot to bring a bathing suit. She went shopping and purchased an expensive suit—the most expensive one in the shop—then informed her new husband, "My sister needs a bathing suit, too. And I think my mother needs one, too."

After returning to New York, the couple moved in with Ruthie's grandmother and aunt, but it wasn't long before Ruthie's grandmother moved out to give Celia and Leo their freedom. Shortly after that, Leo introduced Hela to his friend Joseph, known as Josie, hoping the two would become a couple. Leo had met up with Josie after the war. They knew each other from when they were young people and neighborhood friends, but they hadn't seen each other since Josie, who was a brilliant student, had moved to Warsaw for school. Josie knew everything about everything and read all the time—qualities that Leo assumed would appeal to Hela's own intellectual leanings. Josie would have made a perfect university professor or entrepreneur, but when he immigrated to the US—unlike in Europe, where he had pursued a number of different initiatives—he took someone's advice that it was most important to put your head down and work a steady job. He worked as a salesman in a dry goods store and then as a salesman for Leo's optical business before declaring at age sixty that he had a heart condition and needed to retire.

Ruthie's parents, aunts, uncles, and an extended family of survivors spent enormous amounts of time together, trying to take care of one another. Together, in their little neighborhood in Queens, they created a whole culture of care in all its forms.

CHAPTER 3

And now for my side of the family.

Martin

My father was born in Transylvania, which was part of Hungary at the time and then became part of Romania after World War II. Martin spoke both Hungarian and Romanian fluently. He had two brothers—David and Eliezer—and two sisters—Esther, whose nickname was Koka, and another sister who died in the camps. The siblings' mother had died giving birth to Koka. Afterward, their father remarried, uniting with a lovely woman who brought with her a son. She and her son also did not survive the camps.

At the age of thirteen, Martin was sent to the big city, Budapest, to find a job, earn money, and help support his family. Given the timing of his departure, he did not get to establish much of a relationship with his new stepmother and her son.

It was while working in Budapest as a carpenter that Martin was among those rounded up and transported to a labor camp, and then from the labor camp he was put on one of the trains to the death camps. Unnoticed by the guards, he jumped off the train and eventually made his way back to Budapest. There, he hid along with others in a synagogue. Martin managed to remain safe, but the German soldiers regularly shot and killed many of the Jews around him. While there, he took on the role of sneaking out in the dark of night to carry bodies to makeshift graves.

David and Koka survived the camps. Eliezer lived in the forests of Hungary and fought against the Germans as a partisan. Postwar, Martin located his siblings after seeing their information posted on the doors of the local synagogue.

All of them moved to Israel after the war. Eliezer joined a kibbutz in the north of Israel, called Parod, known for its Jewish Hungarian immigrant culture. Most of the residents there spoke Hungarian, or they spoke Hebrew with Hungarian accents. Eliezer married a woman named Marta and had three children. I remember him visiting us in Giv'atayim when I was just a child. He would bring me almonds still in their shells, and we would sit together, breaking the shells and eating the almonds while he entertained me with lively and interesting stories.

David lived in a religious community next to Haifa, married and had two daughters, and owned a shoe store. Koka lived in Israel for some time. At the time, she qualified as an old spinster, because she didn't marry until she was thirty. When she did finally marry, it was to a Canadian man who brought her back home with him to Canada to live.

Although my father had lost his parents, a sister, and one brother, he had already been living independently since he was sent to Budapest to work. My sense is that, unlike his brothers, my father's desire to travel the world came from having been separated from his family early on. Since the time he'd been a young teenager, he was free to do as he wanted. Then, after the war, he was still alive and still free to act in ways that were deeply enjoyable. Traveling, taking a wife, and building a family—these were the things on which he focused his energy. When my elder sister, Zipi, was born, the nurse came to meet him in the waiting room with the happy news: "It's a girl!" Martin received her warmly and then sat back down in his chair and said, "Maybe I'll wait here a little longer and see if a boy comes out."

Haviva

My mother was from Lithuania. Her father, Meir, owned a factory that produced turpentine, coal, and starch. The Germans wanted to keep the factory functional throughout the war, and because my grandfather was essential to continuing factory operations, he managed to protect his wife, my mother, and her two brothers for quite some time. Through his various connections, Meir kept track of the maneuverings of the Germans. In preparation for hiding his family, he dug a hole—the first of many—under the factory floor.

Meir's is a story with many twists and turns. Zipi remembers that the two of us heard him tell that story when I was about nine years old and she was about thirteen. We also have my grandfather's written attempts to account for that period of time, but even those are not entirely illuminating. In all, he was able to save his children, but not without years of effort either to find or create for them suitable hiding places by building lean-tos, digging holes in floors, creating secret chambers in attic walls, sending them away to different locations in the care of other people, and always paying careful attention to the movements of the Germans.

Zipi reminded me of a story about my grandmother's sister, Michle, handing her child to her husband, jumping into one of the holes that contained my uncles Ben and Ezerkai, and refusing to yield her spot to my grandmother. Michle's husband and child and my grandmother all died shortly thereafter along with others who were rounded up, taken into a nearby field, and shot. After the war, Michle moved to Israel, but my mother and her two brothers found themselves unable to forgive her for her brutal act of self-preservation.

Postwar, Haviva and Martin separately made their way to the same displaced persons camp in Germany. Martin was twenty-six; Haviva was only seventeen. My father was an excellent dancer and a jovial man and easily won Haviva's attention. They married quickly, though Meir and other remaining family on that side refused to attend the wedding. They believed that my mother was too young for Martin and that Martin's experience as a carpenter wasn't a suitable enough profession. Though my grandfather fussed about my mother's marriage to an older man, immediately postwar, he remarried and in so doing created quite a lot of additional friction in the family.

My father had fifty dollars in his pocket and to his name when he, my mother, and my grandfather all moved together to Israel in 1949. They settled in Jaffa, and my father continued to work as a carpenter. He began by working for other people but eventually established an independent business. Actually, he formed a partnership with another carpenter, and they opened a business together. From that first partner forward, every one of my father's business collaborators possessed a noticeable stutter. My mother, who always told people exactly what she thought, recognized the pattern early on and told my father that the reason he kept choosing partners who stuttered was so that he could tell them absolutely anything at all, and they would never come back at him with a coherent reply.

My mother's brother Ezerkai traveled to Israel to see about living there but decided it was not for him. He returned to Europe, and shortly thereafter he and Ben both moved to New York.

Haviva thoroughly enjoyed being a homemaker. In these days and times, I don't know of anyone who says they *want* to be a homemaker. If I were dating now and my date were to tell me she wants to be a homemaker, I would have to seriously reconsider my interest. But in the generation before us, wives were basically instructed not to work. Working was viewed as shameful, an indicator that your family did not have enough money for you to stay at home and focus on caring for the family. Women were told that it was a valuable thing to move to the suburbs, dote on the kids, and cook the casseroles.

My mother was happy to play the role of caregiver, and she was a spectacular cook. For her, food was love, and cooking was her way of opening her heart, and our household, to new cultures and experiences. Long before all the ingredients were easily available and before anyone had access in their homes to cuisines from around the world, Haviva was making the most delicious Chinese, Moroccan, Thai, and Russian dishes. In those days, it was almost impossible to find Chinese spices, but she would seek them out, or she would improvise creative substitutions. The only thing Haviva refused to do in the role of happy homemaker was bite her own tongue. She once explained it to Ruthie like this: "Our father had two sons and then me, and from my earliest days, I would hear him say, 'I had a daughter to take care of me when I get old.' From the time I was ten years old, no one said a nice word to me. Everyone just made demands. So, I coped by becoming brutally honest, telling the people around me the truth whenever I had the opportunity."

Ruthie and I have grown used to telling these stories about our parents—so used to the telling that sometimes it's as if we almost forget just how extraordinary it is that our parents survived and found one another. There were so many split-second decisions and gut-level responses, so many last-minute arrangements and narrow escapes, so many subtleties of subterfuge and quick wit. Making sense of their lives isn't entirely possible, as many of the details remain either hidden from or otherwise impenetrable to us.

But then, of course, in another sense, we have never forgotten, could never forget. Our lives, our children's, and their children's lives—the very fact of us all—are determined, shaded, by their survival.

CHAPTER 4

Those nights when Ruthie was lying in bed uninterested in falling asleep, she would hear her father talking about his early years in New York. Listening to those stories—or, rather, hearing the portions of them that she could make out from her room—made her think, *What a lot of crazy young people!*

I suppose this is correct. Here were groups of teenagers and twentysomethings, many of them totally orphaned, living without a tether in a new world. They were alive. They were free. And they may have gone a little crazy making each other laugh, holding each other close, and living almost as if they were invincible.

When he first came to America, Leo didn't want to live alone—almost no survivor did—so he moved the tenement apartment on Tenth and Second Avenues where Luba's sister Regina and her husband, Ben, lived. There, Leo shared a cramped room with a fellow named Henry, who, though his immigration papers declared otherwise, was actually Ben's twin brother. When Henry was drafted into the Korean War, Leo was aghast. "What the hell are you doing, going to war after you survived?"

"I was drafted" was Henry's only reply.

Henry's experience in the armed forces was short lived. When he arrived at the boat to which he'd been assigned, he was called out of line. Barely five feet tall, Henry was dragging his rifle alongside him, the rifle scraping against the cement. Instead of being shipped off to Korea, Henry was given a different job, served out the entirety of his tenure in that role, and then returned to the apartment and to the room he shared with Leo.

Leo was convinced that Henry needed to get married, but he struggled to find Henry a wife. Henry was a short, slim fellow, and Leo eventually found him a short, tiny survivor named Sonja. They seemed to hit it off, except that Sonja's mother, who had earned the nickname "the general," rejected the pairing.

"Henry, you don't have any money. You cannot marry my daughter, my only child. She's only eighteen. I don't want her marrying some pauper."

To solve that problem, Leo put $10,000 into Henry's bank account. Then, Henry showed the bank passbook to Sonja's mother.

"Ten thousand dollars you have? Oh, absolutely you should marry my Sonja!"

A week later, Henry returned the $10,000. Sonja's mother never knew. Henry got himself work in a garment factory, where he later became a foreman, and he and Sonja had a sixty-year-long marriage.

Leo and his relatives moved to a tenement building on Second Avenue where they lived across the courtyard from one another. The stairwells were tall and narrow, but the men insisted that they didn't need to hire movers whenever they acquired a new piece of furniture. Instead, they devised a pully system for lifting large items through the windows that overlooked the building's courtyard. They were not afraid of anything, not even of how their neighbors would react when a gust of wind caught the underside of a sofa and sent it swinging back and forth between corners of the building, causing it to break every window it hit before crashing to the ground in hundreds of pieces. They just laughed their way from one ridiculous situation to the next.

Leo carried a lot of people on his shoulders—taking care of them financially and emotionally—from his first months in America until the day he died. He took care of the young cousin who escaped Auschwitz with his wife and her sister; he gave extended family the money they needed to start a real estate business in Toronto; he took care of his brother-in-law Josie when, at age sixty, he announced his weak heart and his retirement; and he took care of his brother, Shulim, when after thirty-five years in Argentina he and Luba finally decided to move to New York. Though Shulim did not speak any English, he quickly learned the phrase, "I know, I know!" That one-liner worked well enough when Leo put him to work making deliveries and doing odd jobs.

The telling thing about Leo is this: He was very driven to play the hand that had been dealt him in life, to support his family, and to transform suffering into success. In the camp, Shulim had carried Leo; in America, Leo saw it as his purpose to carry on his shoulders a whole host of others. He understood supporting other survivors as his true task, and both he and Celia were happy that they were in a position to be able to take care of people. When a relative or friend needed money, they would simply go to the bank, withdraw the cash, and show up at the doorstep of the person who'd called on them. For them, generosity was a sign of a successful life.

Taking care of people's emotional needs was more difficult, but they kept at it. Ruthie's mother was totally devoted to caring for her sister, sister-in-law Luba, and mother. She did what she could, even when there was not much that could be done.

Leo looked at his past with clear eyes but felt compelled to do everything he could to enjoy the life he had and ensure that his children would enjoy and appreciate their own lives by living them fully. That meant Ruthie and Sarena, her sister, grew up spending holidays, parts of summers, and many, many family celebrations surrounded by their cousins—and the cousins of cousins. To this day, we join Ruthie's cousins and their families for all the big gatherings commemorating life's transitions, and her dearest cousins Rhoda and Jay celebrate all the major holidays with us.

Leo and Celia showed Ruthie and Sarena how to live generously and openly, even in the aftermath of incomprehensible catastrophe. They were good to everyone, the best hosts, and successful most of all at being human.

CHAPTER 5

Everyone handled their pain differently. And so, every family of survivors had a different experience.

Two people with very similar experiences during the war could easily live very different lives afterward. Some needed to talk about what they went through; others refused. Some were much more damaged psychologically, suffering mental breakdowns and other illnesses; others found suitable enough mechanisms for coping. Some people eked out their existence; others ran toward life with deepened enthusiasm. Every household was unique. But no household was without its secrets.

In my household, no one spoke of the Holocaust. When I had a school assignment requiring me to discuss it, I had to force some stories out of my parents. Zipi and I had what could be referred to as "normal" childhoods, except, of course, that we lived in Israel, which, in addition to the collective trauma of the survivor population, had its own persistent issues and tensions. I was born in the middle of a war in 1956, and during my youth, there was the Six-Day War in 1967, then the Yom Kippur War in 1973, and in between those, a couple of other smaller wars.

For a middle-income family, my parents did amazingly well. Not only was Martin a fantastic dancer; he was also an incredibly talented carpenter. He excelled at complicated woodworking projects and was tapped to work on synagogues and other intricate carpentry and architectural projects. We kids did not miss out on experiences, and Martin and Haviva were able to do whatever they wanted. I mentioned earlier that my parents settled in Jaffa, a less expensive alternative to Tel Aviv, where they secured a small place that they shared with my grandfather, his wife, her daughter, and that daughter's husband. After a couple of other moves, and by the time I was in my early twenties serving in the army, my parents settled into a house in a fancy neighborhood in Tel Aviv. They also bought some land in Tel Aviv where now stands a set of apartments that my sister and I own.

That said, there were also subtle signs, cracks in the behavior of those around us, that betrayed wounds unhealed.

My mother, for example, was carefully accumulating food all the time. And she always, always answered the telephone as if each call were about a most urgent matter. She was much more comfortable staying within the walls of the house than she was going out. My parents may have traveled around the world, but that was entirely my father's doing—ensuring that my mother not only got out of the house but also got to see as many other places and countries as possible.

In Israel, as in many other places around the world, when you are a carpenter, you are typically paid in cash. Whenever he worked for other people, my father always resented that the employee gifts he received on holidays were actual things—like bottles of wine or boxes of chocolates. To him, cash was both the most honest and the most valuable gift. While my father valued cash above other forms of payment, he also spent a considerable amount of effort being petrified of the Israeli IRS. Ruthie finds this hilarious, because until quite recently, the IRS in Israel was a bit of a joke. Nevertheless, my father remained vigilant. When the IRS hosted an appreciation event for small business owners who were exceptionally good about reporting their income and paying their taxes, my father was among those invited. Of the big stack of cash he carried with him, he reported, "It was burning a hole in my pocket!"

One of the classic stories of our family recounts a short trip that my father and mother took from Jaffa to Tel Aviv and back—about four miles each way. My father drove his motorcycle with my mother holding on to him from behind. On the way back, Martin arrived in Jaffa only to realize that Haviva was no longer with him on the back of the bike. He turned around, retraced his route, and found her sitting and waiting for him by the side of the road, right where she'd fallen off the motorcycle without his having noticed.

In a sense, that silly obliviousness is similar to a story I can tell from my own youth, when our family lived in a third-floor walk-up. I remember coming home one afternoon to a room full of neighbors laughing merrily and enjoying one another's company. Apparently, from her perch in the kitchen, my mother had attempted to place a call but hadn't done so successfully. My father, thinking he'd heard the phone ring in another room, picked up the receiver and started up a conversation with the person on the other line. It took a full fifteen minutes before either of them realized that they were talking on the same phone line—to one another.

With Ruthie's parents, things were a bit different. In the right company, Ruthie's father would have talked about the Holocaust every day. But he never shared a story with Ruthie one on one, and her mother never spoke a word about any of it—she would even leave the room when those late-night conversations around the kitchen table turned to the recounting of traumatic experiences. Ruthie remembers her aunt Luba saying, "None of us are normal. We can't be normal." For all their scars, Leo and Celia were high-functioning individuals and a highly functional couple. Their commitment to supporting others was for them a kind of coping mechanism.

Leo spoke English poorly, but he read the *New York Times* newspaper—or, as he pronounced it, the "pay-po"—from cover to cover every single day in an attempt to understand what was going on around him at all times. He smiled all the time and spoke with a thick Yiddish accent; these superficial features could give the impression that he didn't pay much attention to the world at large, but in fact he was vigilant—very aware and very attuned to other people's experiences.

Ruthie's mother, with her quiet, polished, almost regal presence, may have maintained a certain old-fashioned concern for propriety, but both she and Leo put their best efforts into being full participants in the modern world. Both were committed to ensuring that Ruthie and her sister went to the best schools and understood that they could do anything they wanted as long as they put their minds to it.

Both Ruthie and I noticed that a lot of survivors carried their past experiences into their parenting by always admonishing their children, "*You* have to eat everything on your plate, because *we* were starving," or "*You* have to enjoy this privilege, because *we* were suffering and miserable." But our parents never spoke to us this way. They did not envy their children. Instead, they thought our childhoods should be free from *their* pasts. I was always encouraged to do my own thing; Ruthie was always encouraged to explore her talents. For both of us—Ruthie in New York City and me in Tel Aviv—our friends were always welcome in our family homes. Both sets of parents liked facilitating other people's enjoyment; they were able to take pleasure in the silliness of carefree children and the occasional drama of their childhood troubles.

Every now and then, Ruthie's father would say to her that he was born in the wrong time and the wrong place and that she was born in the right time and the right place, so she was lucky. But he never said it as a way of chastising her, never used that insight to say, "You don't appreciate what you have," or "You'll never understand."

Our parents saw to it that we were given the foundations and the experience we needed to be successful ourselves, and they instilled in us the significance of continuing the traditions belonging to our Jewish heritage and the importance of making sure we share those traditions with our own children, and that our children remember the value of sharing them with theirs, for generations to come.

Ruthie and I carry with us an understanding of the value of investing everything in our kids and our grandkids the way our parents invested everything in us. From childhoods spent watching and listening, we learned that our relatives could all have died, that there might have been no continuation of our families going forward. The generation before us had been hunted, so they were focused on survival—my mother accumulating food and my father with the cash burning holes in his pockets; Ruthie's father's vigilance and her mother's quiet refusal to discuss the past. They celebrated life when and as they could, and their offspring were to them the most fragile, precious gifts, each one a literal miracle. By contrast, our generation is focused on continuation of that lineage. Our obsession with our kids is a reflection, an outgrowth, of the prior generation's astonishment at their own survival. They made it; they had children, and as their children, we see it as our task to preserve and continue what they started, to ensure that the light is not extinguished and that the generations after us can thrive.

Once, while riding in an elevator, Ruthie overheard one woman say to another, "I don't know how I'm going to manage paying for my kids' tuition, for their sports activities, for this and that …" As the woman continued listing expenses, a man standing opposite interjected, "You're not Jewish. You don't have to do everything for your kids!"

Ruthie thought to herself, *You know what? He's kind of right.* We were raised to think that family was everything, that having and rearing children holds the deepest significance. Our own knowledge that our families experienced something horrific has affected our life choices and our attitudes about living. And our kids are at the center of all that; continuing to build and maintain a strong economic base so the next generation can thrive is a big part of what we believe we owe to those who came before us in light of both their suffering and their remarkable fortitude.

✻

CHAPTER 6

Ruthie and I didn't date until we were in our mid-twenties, but we met when we were just ten years old.

Ruthie's mother, Celia, and my aunt Ruth, my uncle Ben's wife, were best friends. Though they lived a couple of blocks away from each other, the two women talked on the phone in Polish for hours every evening. Because they were so close, they visited Israel together, and that's how my family got to know Ruthie's family.

It was both a common thing to visit people's relatives while visiting Israel and a big deal to make such a considerable trip. So, of course, my family has pictures and home movies of Ruthie and her family's visit. There's one movie of us all saying goodbye to one another at the airport. Those were the days when people accompanied their visitors to the airport and lingered to witness their departures. The movie shows my family standing on the airport terrace, watching Ruthie's family walk up the stairs to board their plane. Ruthie's mother always dressed her girls in tip-top fashions, and so we have this lasting record of Ruthie and Sarena looking like perfect dolls.

A family photo of that same event hangs in our apartment today. In the picture, I am standing just left of center looking out at the camera, and Ruthie is standing on the far right-hand side of the group.

If one looks with a discerning eye, it's quite possible to see that Ruthie is looking over at me. "Even then," I tell everyone who visits, "she was absolutely crazy about me."

I can't say that I had the same effect on other people during my early years. I was considered the black sheep in my immediate family. My sister was a straight-A student, and I was a straight-F student, totally uninterested in my studies. Zipi cruised through school. I didn't do homework, except on a handful of occasions. In a family where education was considered the most important thing, I was intent on being the rebel, the clown who announced that he didn't care about all that. Every time I'd get a report card, there would be a ceremony in our household. My mother—a very smart woman in her own right—would see it and be beside herself, not knowing what to do in response. Next, she'd show the report to my father, who imme-diately knew what to do. He'd get out his belt and come running after me. But I never received my punishment. I was too fast on my feet and would wind through the apartment dodging couches and tables, escaping to the street before he could reach me.

Although you could say that there's a war in Israel nearly every five minutes, not all of them have the same resonance. I clearly remember the Six-Day War of 1967, which occurred when I was just eleven years old. It began with a surprise invasion. All the sirens went off, and all of us kids were rushed out of our classrooms and into nearby shelters. My first reaction was to feel lucky; once again, I hadn't completed my homework, and on this day it absolutely didn't matter.

My next reaction was to feel completely unnerved. As a kid, espe-cially the kid of Holocaust survivors, being in a war and not knowing what's going to happen is … well, let me say that it was an experience that has stayed with me. In those early hours, I felt thankful that my father had only recently cut his hand at work and therefore did not have to serve as an ambulance driver on the front lines. Still, I couldn't help but notice how vulnerable we all were, how little we could do to protect ourselves except make our way to shelters and into basements. In this war, as would be the case in others, Israel was like David fighting Goliath—a trio of surrounding countries (Egypt, Jordan, and Syria) whose might threatened to destroy our country altogether. The siren sounds persisted, and a flurry of ominous radio reporting updated us daily.

Israel is a tiny country, with neighboring countries always threatening "to kick the Jews into the sea." We didn't know it at the time, but Israel had actually started this war with a preemptive strike that took out all the surrounding countries' air forces. We controlled the sky, and within six days, we took a big piece of land from Syria in the north as well as the Sinai desert and the West Bank, including Jerusalem. That our forces had succeeded so quickly against all three countries put Israel on the map and granted it, if only temporarily, popularity around the world.

At a young age, I lived both the distress of that war and the euphoria of its aftermath, when Israel solidified its reputation on the world stage as a power to be reckoned with and then worked to fortify its borders. For a while thereafter, it felt good to be an Israeli, good to be a Jewish family living in Israel. We might not have been able to rely on other countries to help us, but we proved that we could stand our own ground, that our armed forces were strong.

By the time of the Yom Kippur War, I was a senior in high school. I had improved my grades a bit after being pulled aside by my teacher during the first quarter of my sophomore year. There were fifteen subjects, and I had earned thirteen F's plus fair enough scores in gymnastics and pre-army training. I congratulated myself, noting that it took real talent to get so many F's. But then the teacher suggested that I focus on putting some effort into subjects that I liked, because there was no other way I would make it to the next grade. That conversation was a wake-up call for me, and I decided to do as she suggested. The second quarter of sophomore year, I earned only six F's and then finished the year with only two, thereby skidding through to junior status.

The Yom Kippur War was another surprise war—this time started when Syria and Egypt invaded Israel. It shouldn't have been a surprise war, because Israel had received warnings. But we had also summarily dismissed those warnings. I suppose our leaders refused to believe that Egypt had the nerve to attack a country with such a well-fortified army. The intent of the invading countries was, in fact, to surprise Israel on a national holiday and thereby slow our response time. That turned out to be a strategic mistake, because on Yom Kippur, nobody travels—nobody even leaves the house—so there are barely any cars on the roads. Instead of being slowed in its response, Israel got its reserves in place quicker than it would have on nearly any other day of the year.

A lot of my friends were drafted. I was seventeen then, and if I had been just a year older, I also would have been called to participate. Instead, my classmates and I volunteered to work on behalf of employees who had to leave their jobs to fight. I worked in a milk factory and was paid with products. I brought home more yogurts, cheeses, creams, and milk than even my food-hoarding mother knew what to do with.

That was the war in which we came closest to losing our country. Syria went into the Golan Heights and conquered almost all the lands that we had won in 1967. The Egyptians took over major parts of the Sinai desert with minimal resistance. Our invaders were so shocked at how easy a time they were having that they paused their attacks for a bit, giving Israeli forces the opportunity to regroup. The stories coming from the front were dire. There was no news about our winning any fights—only updates about holding back or slowing the onslaught.

Sensing the direness of the threat, then–prime minister Golda Meir turned to America's then-president Nixon, who didn't want to support Israel in its fight, and she calmly and publicly declared that Israel had opened its nuclear silos. When Meir warned, "Israel will not go alone!" Nixon finally responded by offering needed aid. Still, it was a long war with a lot of casualties. If the 1967 war had left us with joy and a strong sense of our military force, the 1973 war reminded us that we had formidable enemies intent on destroying us. Both wars required us to take note that we couldn't count on anyone but ourselves to defend us. With that insight renewed, Israel developed its own manufacturing capacity for weapons, tanks, and drones. We were still a small country, but this time we would ensure that we had a big bite.

That year, I finally made an arrangement with my parents: if I didn't get any F's for the entire year, they would send me to Europe for two months in the summertime.

I got to take that trip.

While I was having those formative experiences in Israel, Ruthie and her sister were growing up in a neighborhood in Queens populated by a lot of Holocaust survivors. For a good bit of her childhood, Ruthie believed that all people in all neighborhoods were identical to hers—that the whole world was composed of survivor communities.

Her family summered in the Catskills, but instead of staying in the bungalow colonies, which Leo thought were ugly, he would gather an entire group of friends and their children and rent part of a small hotel for six weeks. The kids would enjoy day camp, the women would enjoy dance and other lessons, and the men would come out on the weekends to spend time away from work and with their families. Those summers were fun for everyone, a period during the year when even the adults did quite a lot of relaxing and celebrating. They were alive, they were free, they had families, and they committed to having a good time.

By the time Ruthie was about eleven years old, the Catskills gatherings had ended. She would spend the next five summers at sleepaway camp. She was not a great camper in terms of being nice to her counselors or being interested in sports—including swimming, which she truly hated—but she had the best time at camp, just loved the entire experience, and made some lasting friendships there. The young people attended classes in the mornings and recreational activities in the afternoons, and Ruthie worked with campers with disabilities as part of her service. It was a Jewish camp with very few survivors' kids, so for Ruthie it was a big moment of exposure to the kids of Jewish people who had emigrated to the US well before the war.

School was always easy for Ruthie. She spent very little time on homework but always made her parents happy with how well she did academically. Instead of studying in the evenings, she would set her hair, watch episodes of *The Mary Tyler Moore Show*, and stay up late talking on the phone with her friends. When she was seventeen, her parents sent her to the Weizmann Institute of Science in Israel. And when the researchers there told her that part of her responsibility involved killing mice by snapping their necks, she said to them, "I'm sorry, but this is just not for me." She stuck it out, did not kill any mice, and got to meet kids from all over the world.

The summer before Ruthie went to Weizmann, she visited a great-aunt and uncle in Israel who were ultraorthodox. In those days, the electronics coming into Israel were very elementary, and you could not bring in any items without paying taxes to the hilt. But before she made that trip, Ruthie decided that her relatives needed a television and that she would bring them a small black-and-white unit to enjoy.

She had a brilliant plan for getting the TV through customs: place it in the center of her suitcase, pack her underwear all around it, and then put a poster of Elvis on top.

When the customs officers opened her suitcase, they spent some minutes talking to one another in Hebrew, thinking that Ruthie couldn't understand what they were saying.

"Who is this idiot, thinking she can bring in a television?" Then in broken English, they said to her, "You're not allowed to bring a TV."

To which she responded, "You want an American to survive an entire summer without television?"

They exchanged glances, and one of them said in Hebrew, "You know what? Just let her go."

Her great-aunt and uncle were in total shock when she unpacked the TV. Here was their niece bringing them a gift of something they were forbidden to possess. But once they discovered they could hide the television in a dining room cabinet, they acknowledged that it was a great gift.

People tell Ruthie that she's an interesting combination of the old world and the new. When I asked her if she thought that was true, she said to me, "Well, I know my place in Jewish history, and I understand the significance of family more than many people do. We have to stick together more than a lot of people do. Our family is my overriding interest and concern, and our sons and their families are my life."

Personally, I think that's the extent of the old world in her. Because the rest of Ruthie's story is thoroughly modern: advanced schooling, an interesting career path, and professional experiences that run parallel with mine.

CHAPTER 7

fter I graduated high school, it was time for me to go into the Israel Defense Forces. A lot of my friends and I made the transition from high school into the army pondering the fact that we all knew someone who had died in the recent war. We wondered out loud about our own chances.

I'd always wanted to be a pilot—for all the wrong reasons. First, there is a saying in Israel: "The best, to the air force," and I considered myself among the best. Second, I had a strong impression that women liked men who were in the air force and that they especially liked and admired pilots.

When it came time to apply to the Israeli Air Force, I misrepresented myself on my application form. In response to the question "Have you ever fainted?" I answered no, even though I had once fainted from sunstroke during a high school–sponsored trip to the desert. I didn't believe that little detail should in any way impede my participation.

I was of course thrilled when, after a series of tests and interviews, I was accepted into the pilot course. The way that program worked, after two years of coursework, I would have to sign on for an additional five years of service. I was willing to agree to that time commitment—because I would be flying jets and be considered the

THE COURAGE TO CONTINUE

best of the best! It was a boost to my self-esteem to get accepted to the most prestigious program and a comfort to know what the next seven years of my life would look like.

A few friends started the pilot course along with me, and the tremendous amount of studying required to make it through the two years of training quickly became clear to me. As we know, my academic career up to that point had not been stellar, and I wondered to myself whether I would survive long enough to become a pilot.

After the initial two weeks of basic training, 50 percent of the people who had been accepted for the pilot course were let go. In those two weeks, the air force completed all its assessments and research, and my superiors found out about my lie after accessing my school records.

They offered me an alternative. Because I had not been honest on my application form, there was no way I could continue with the current training. But if I wanted to reapply in one year, they would once again accept me into the pilot course.

It's true that I had wondered about my prospects overall. But being turned away just then, at the very start, and for what seemed like such a stupid reason? That was devastating. I hadn't envisioned an alternative path, and I struggled to wrap my head around the idea of delaying the start of my service for an entire year. Instead of waiting to reapply, I made the decision to accept what had happened and focus on finishing my service. I would have to survive being in the armed forces without getting to enjoy flying around in the sky or going around Tel Aviv identifying myself as a pilot. Honestly, once becoming a pilot was off the table, staying alive became *the* key factor influencing any future decisions about my assignment.

In light of that aim, I thought about the Israeli Navy's participation in the 1973 war, actively fighting other missile boats with far superior capabilities than their own. No one in the navy had died in that war. No one had been injured. To the contrary, the navy had experienced some big wins.

I decided that being assigned to a missile boat in the navy would offer me the best chance of survival. So, to the navy I applied.

Next, I learned that if I wanted to be in the navy, I had to volunteer to join. When I did that, they actually had to check to see if they could take me. The reason was that people who flunked out of the pilot course are considered command material and expected to volunteer at the officer level in the navy. But I'd learned that taking the officer pathway would require an additional three years of service, and I most definitely didn't want that. Thankfully, the navy had not yet met its quota for people who could enlist without also becoming an officer. That meant I could get in under the wire.

The navy sent the volunteers on a weeklong test of compatibility, during which they put all of us on a missile boat without any training whatsoever.

I spent the entire week throwing up. I mapped out the locations of all the puke buckets, and at all times I was keenly aware of the precise distance between me and any bucket on the boat. We disembarked at the end of the week, but even standing on the pier, I still felt as if the whole world was spinning.

Back at the base, I sat across from the officer who had supervised the test. He was looking at a report detailing how I had survived the week. "Do you still want to be in the navy?" he asked.

"I am going to shock you," I said, "because I am going to stay."

I eventually adjusted to living on a boat. I trained to shoot the canons and missiles, later earning the post of sergeant major. Once each year, we invited family and friends to visit us at the base in Haifa, and we would give everyone a brief tour of the missile boat and then take them sailing for an hour. The day before my family came to visit me for the first time, there was an attack on Israel from Lebanon, and my boat participated in the retaliatory effort. I was the guy who shot the cannon, which meant that I sat in a booth above the bridge using very strong binoculars to help me take aim at our targets. I shot 150 straight shells. The following day, we had a rough hour at sea with everyone's friends and family on board—and nearly all the guests were unwell at some point. But during the trip, the commander spoke about our efforts and highlighted our successful participation in the fighting the prior evening. He even noted that the paint on the cannon had melted from all the shooting.

When we returned to shore, my family turned to me with looks of deep admiration in their eyes. I felt proud that I had been active in the successful retaliation effort. And so, I was a bit surprised when I discovered the source of their esteem: "How can you do this, be on a boat all the time with all the waves? It's unbelievable!"

Our missile boat had about forty people on board, which meant that it was a big boat for Israel but a small boat by the standards of other countries' navies. Most of the people on our boat were either Moroccans or Sephardic Jews, and I struggled in my first couple of months to eat all the spicy foods they were preparing—I hardly ate anything until my gut finally adjusted. By the time I was put on kitchen duty to serve as a sous-chef, I was happy to learn how to prepare all the food I was eating. A couple of those dishes I still cook for the family today.

I am proud of my service in the navy and the operations in Libya and Lebanon in which I participated. We did a lot of good things, including stopping terrorists that were approaching the Israeli border. When my conscription ended after three years, I became part of the reserve, where I served until I turned fifty. And I made friends for life.

Not long after I entered the reserve, I was called to transfer into the infantry and report back to the military base at Haifa. A friend of mine suggested that I write to the head of the navy asking permission to stay with that organization. I suppose that was my very first lesson in negotiating. I have to say that I was somewhat surprised when that worked, and I learned that asking was a critical part of figuring out whether something is, in fact, possible.

I had entered the navy and then requested to stay with the navy as a reservist because I wanted to serve in an environment that was competitive but also safe. Thankfully, that turned out to be my experience. But it was not the experience of everyone in my family.

My uncle Eliezer—who lived on a kibbutz and always brought almonds in their shells whenever he visited—and his wife, Marta, had three children: two daughters and one son. Their son, my cousin Gidon, was the prince of the family—a born leader and a big thinker, very opinionated and very charismatic. In his early teens, he was already successfully managing the cotton field operations on the kibbutz. In the army, Gidon served in one of the elite commando units and had been put in charge of a missile launcher. During a training session, the missile he was working with did not shoot. So, Gidon decided he would take the missile back to his dormitory where he could work on fixing it. When he did, the missile exploded, and he died. He was in his early twenties, just a couple of years older than me.

At the time, my aunt Koka, who was living in Canada with her husband, was on her way to Israel for her first visit in many years. My uncle Eliezer was already in Tel Aviv to welcome Koka. I was supposed to take leave the next day, and the whole family was planning on enjoying some quality time together.

I will never forget Gidon's death. It happened during my first year in the navy. I was on guard duty on the boat, excited to leave the next day, when I got a phone call saying that my parents were at the gate. Eliezer had been with them when he got the call that his son had died in the explosion. I got permission to leave the boat immediately, and we all traveled to the kibbutz for the funeral.

Losing Gidon was horrible for all of us. In a sense, his death destroyed that whole family. They never recuperated. Eliezer and Marta walked to Gidon's grave every day, and for the rest of their lives, to visit with them was to feel the void created by his absence.

Gidon and I had grown up close, even spent summers together at the kibbutz. Even at my young age, I understood that nearly every family loses a child in the fight for Israel. But Gidon was the first loss in our family. After him, the only remaining male child in the Fisher family was me.

CHAPTER 8

While I was busy serving in the Israeli armed forces, Ruthie spent some time volunteering on a kibbutz. She came to help the state of Israel after the Yom Kippur War, but she didn't last long at the task. Her first job was picking onions. I should say that onion picking is absolutely horrible. Only the American volunteers and the Arabs are assigned to pick onions. For the Israelis, it's too difficult a job.

I remember that when I finished my service in the Israeli army, the first thing I did was apply for and earn a job leading a group of American kids like Ruthie, who'd come to Israel for a week at a time to help and get to know the country. One of the highlights of my job was encouraging the group I led to spend their first three days on the kibbutz working like crazy and earning the reputation of being excellent at their tasks. "Then, on the back end," I would encourage them, "you can relax while all the other groups have to prove themselves."

Ruthie didn't have me as her guide on the kibbutz, so of course she hated her experience. From there, she went off to college at Johns Hopkins University in Baltimore. Nearly all the children of her parents' friends went to Queens College in New York. Going to Queens College was a given among the children of survivors who grew up where Ruthie did. Everyone's thinking went something like this: *Education is important, so you go to college to get an advanced education. Queens College is right here where we all live, and it's cheap, so you go to get your advanced education at Queens College.*

But Ruthie's father, in his typically generous and forward-thinking fashion, said to her and her sister, "I want you to go to the best schools you can, and I will pay the tuition." Leo wanted them to take that extra step, to get an *excellent* education. So Ruthie went to Johns Hopkins with the assumption that her career options entailed becoming a doctor, a lawyer, or an accountant. She started out in the premed program but didn't like it, didn't even like the very idea of accounting, and so settled on a major in international relations.

When Ruthie went away to college, her parents moved from Queens to Great Neck. Ruthie's father, as comfortable as he was in Queens, always had a vision of having a nicer home. He was constantly thinking about how to put his family in a better position and wanted them to enjoy the fruits of his business success.

As was their habit when it came to communicating about big purchases, Leo said to Celia, "Go buy a house," and she did. She went out, saw something she liked, and purchased it on the spot. Then the two of them called the pay phone in the hallway of Ruthie's dormitory to tell her that they were moving. They ended up loving Great Neck, even though continuing to see their old friends was no longer as easy as stepping outside for a walk across the street or around the block.

When Ruthie looks back on it now, she says that her parents were brave to make that move. They went from a large community of survivors into an even larger community of American Jews with no Holocaust background.

There were, of course, noticeable differences between the Queens and Great Neck communities. In Great Neck, when the rabbi complained to Leo that he was spending all his time in synagogue talking to whomever was sitting next to him, Leo answered, "If I wanted to pray, I would stay at home. I come here to talk, not to pray." At the synagogue in Queens, everyone talked a lot, but the synagogue in Great Neck was more modern, more disciplined. But that didn't stop Leo from making the most of his social time.

Great Neck is also where Ruthie's mother started playing bridge and indulging her more creative side, doing things like sewing fashionable dresses and upholstering the walls. When Ruthie encouraged her mother to take a class or two to explore her artistic talents, Celia refused. Eventually, she did take one class—a course in CPR—after deciding that she needed to know what to do in case of an emergency. The day she finished the class, Celia came home and announced to Leo that she had graduated. He threw himself on the floor, pretending that he needed CPR right there and then.

Ruthie was there, which means that she was witness to what happened next. Without missing a beat, Celia gracefully stepped right over Leo and continued talking.

Ruthie finished her undergraduate education in three years, and when she graduated, she applied and was accepted to law school at New York University. But instead of starting her legal education there, and instead of asking to defer her admission for a year, she decided she should try going to law school in Israel at the Hebrew University of Jerusalem. Ruthie had always imagined she would live in Israel eventually, and this seemed as good an opportunity as any to see what that felt like.

Ruthie's first year in law school at Hebrew University was rough. She wasn't that interested in her courses, she could sense that her professors were trying to "encourage" her—as the only American taking law school courses in Hebrew—to give correct answers on exams, and she was terribly lonely. Everyone she knew in Israel lived in Tel Aviv, including the great-aunt and uncle with whom she had visited when she went to the Weizman Institute and who still made good use of the television set she had gifted them.

Ruthie stuck it out in Jerusalem for a year before leaving. Toward the end of her second semester, she had a conversation with her dean during which he encouraged her to return to the States and reapply to NYU.

In that year when Ruthie was at law school in Israel, since we were both generally in the same place at the same time, she and I talked quite a bit. I remember at one point my mother asking why Ruthie was calling me regularly. When I heard myself answer, "Ma, she's lonely!" I decided to take my friend Doron with me for a weekend visit to Jerusalem. Of course, I wanted to look impressive, so I wore my navy whites.

What I remember of that weekend is two tragedies occurred— only one of which I was able to recognize in the moment.

First, on the very day Doron and I went to spend time with Ruthie, two Israeli Air Force helicopters collided in an accident, and many soldiers died in the crash. A lot of those soldiers had been with me in the initial pilot training class that I ended up leaving. In all, thirty of them died that day. It wasn't lost on me that I could have been in one of those helicopters.

Second, and you'll hopefully recall that I was only about twenty years old at the time, our visit with Ruthie did not go well. We arrived on Friday and had dinner, and everything seemed good. I even felt there might be a bit of romance between me and Ruthie. Then Doron and I learned that one of our favorite soccer players would be participating in a game in Jerusalem on Saturday afternoon. We could not believe our good luck! We woke up on Saturday morning and had breakfast with

Ruthie, and then Doron and I went off to the game—thrilled by the coincidence of our being in Jerusalem to witness the event.

Afterward, the three of us had a plan to drive back to Tel Aviv, where Ruthie was going to visit one of her friends.

We stopped for hummus at a midpoint along the way. When we got back in the car, Doron and I started comparing notes about the soccer game, our good luck being in Jerusalem, and all the great plays we'd witnessed. Somewhere between the hummus stop and our arrival in Tel Aviv ... well, I don't know how exactly to describe it except to say that Ruthie had a meltdown.

If I haven't said it yet, Ruthie is one of those even-keeled people who exudes a remarkable amount of patience—right up until she doesn't.

She started screaming at us about how we'd left her for hours after coming to town to spend the day with her. And then, in no uncertain terms, she told us to pull the car over to the side of the road. She was getting out, right then and there, because she'd had enough.

If there was one thing we did understand in that moment, it was that we should obey her.

I pulled over, and by the time the car reached the side of the road, Ruthie had the door open and was already securing a foothold by which to propel herself onto the street.

She slammed the door shut and walked away.

I looked over at Doron, wide eyed, shrugged my shoulders, and resumed the drive.

Ruthie was perfectly comfortable having been released from hearing us drone on and on about the game. She found a bus stop and made her way to the friend she was planning to visit that evening.

Had there been an opportunity for romance between us, that twenty-four-hour visit had both raised the question and firmly answered it in the negative.

CHAPTER 9

When I finished my service and entered the navy reserves, I applied to university. My grades alone wouldn't have gotten me admitted, but I scored high on the standardized intelligence tests and was accepted to Tel Aviv University to study economics. My parents did not expect much. I remember my mother's words: "Why are you going to the university? It's going to be a waste of money!"

I flunked my first year, but for a relatively good reason. About six weeks prior to finals, I was called to reserve duty for an operation in Lebanon. I served for thirty days and came back to campus during the two weeks leading up to exams.

When I didn't do well on the exams, I was offered the option to retake them. Instead, I decided to see about getting a degree in the US.

I had two reasons for making that decision. The first was that I was eager to earn a degree as quickly as possible, and it seemed there were more opportunities to do this in the US than in Israel. The second was that I had been involved with a girl on and off for about three years. We were stuck in a deeply destructive relationship. Honestly, it wasn't hard to see that we were wrong for one another, constantly pushing each other's buttons and getting into big fights.

Quitting university, breaking off that relationship, and leaving Israel altogether seemed like the appropriate next steps for me. Plus, with my uncles living in New York, I would have a soft landing in a foreign country.

My friend Mayer and I moved to New York City together, both of us just twenty-three years old. We had met in the navy, working together on missile boats. The two of us made our way to New York on visas that allowed us to be in the country for just six months to learn the English language.

I decided that in the US, I wouldn't study economics anymore but rather something that would get me a job fast. So, I chose computer science, and though I applied and was accepted at both Queens College and the New York Institute of Technology, I thought NYIT would be the better option. That school offered me the most transferable degree credit for my experience in the Israeli army. At NYIT, I could complete a degree in about two and a half years.

In New York, I lived in the refinished basement of my uncle Ben and aunt Ruth's place. You'll recall that my aunt talked daily with Ruthie's mother—the two were the best of friends. So, my aunt asked Celia to ask Ruthie to talk me into going to Queens College instead of NYIT. I remember that phone call, Ruthie trying to convince me that Queens was a better school and that getting a degree from a better school would serve me well in the future. I could tell that she wasn't just dutifully following my aunt's instructions; she genuinely cared and wanted what was best for me.

There was good reason for me to trust Ruthie's recommendations, given her understanding of the scene in New York and in America more generally. But I wasn't listening.

I chose NYIT.

Here's the truly surprising thing: studying computer science changed me. Or it might be more accurate to say that I changed once I started studying computer science. I had always liked playing video games, and it turned out that studying computer science was, for me, similar to playing those games—it was both fun and relatively easy.

Without much effort, I became a straight-A student.

You should have seen my mother's face when she learned about my success in school. She could not understand it. Here was a guy who eventually—and barely—made it through high school with a C average who was now decidedly an A student.

Growing up, I had imagined that eventually I would come into my own and build a successful business that I would own. I especially wanted to be independent, in control of my own journey and my own success. In high school, my sister, Zipi, was hardworking and always did well academically. We went to the same elementary and high schools four years apart, and our parents had very different experiences coming to our teacher-parent conferences. I remember my mother telling me that when she arrived for Zipi's conferences, the teacher would say something like, "Mrs. Fisher, you don't need to be here. Your daughter is doing extremely well." But when she arrived for my conferences, the teachers would always begin, "Mrs. Fisher, please take a chair. We have a lot to talk about." From this, I learned that at some point I would have to be a bit more like Zipi in order to become successful.

Imagine not just my mother's surprise but also my own when I finally found a degree program and a field of study that I liked and that was unquestionably easy for me. My parents had always said that I was creative and social, that my mind was working all the time, and now it finally seemed like I was setting myself up to have a future, maybe even a career.

Toward the end of the six months that Mayer and I spent learning English, I had both started my new degree program and found myself a job that would enable me to stay in the country. Both Mayer and I had applied, but only I got work as a security guard for EL AL Israel Airlines at JFK Airport. What today we take to be standard processes—being asked if your suitcase has been under your supervision or if anyone has given you something to hold for them, going through a security checkpoint, and so on—in those days was really only typical protocol for EL AL.

The job didn't pay well, but it was perfect for a student: the hours were flexible, and I got a free ticket to Israel once a year. Most importantly, that job also changed my visa status. I'd come to the US on a limited-time visa for a specific purpose, but the airline gave me a diplomatic visa during the time I worked for them.

Mayer's story was different: he worked illegally at a gas station for almost a year before getting hired on at EL AL and changing his visa status. From there, he went off to Las Vegas to earn a degree in hotel management and then eventually settled in … Idaho.

By the time I started making my way in New York, Ruthie was dating a guy—a tall, boring accountant. Ruthie even tried to set me up with one of her friends so that we could go on double dates. I went on a couple of those double dates, so I know what I'm talking about when I say that Ruthie's guy was boring. I don't remember much about the dates Ruthie arranged for me, but what I do remember is that I had some lessons to learn about clothing myself appropriately in America.

On our first double date, we went to Windows on the World at the top of the World Trade Center, where it was required that the men wear blazers. Now, in Israel, we don't really do blazers, so I had to ask my uncle Ezerkai for help. He gave me one of his son's old jackets—a very bold, colorful plaid—that, Ruthie reminds me to this day, looked more than a bit ridiculous. Before another date, I went shopping with my aunt Ruth, who herself wasn't a very good shopper, and we bought me a raincoat. When I showed up to meet Ruthie wearing the coat, she nearly dropped to the floor laughing. My aunt had helped me select a *women's* raincoat.

While my choice of outerwear certainly nabbed Ruthie's attention, that's clearly not what ultimately lured her to me. She also wasn't at all impressed by the fact that when I came to the US, I was going to school, going to work, and then going out expressly to have fun. Mayer was extremely charming, and women seemed to be drawn to him like butterflies alighting on a precious bloom. I enjoyed being with *that* guy and only occasionally hung out with Ruthie and her boring accountant boyfriend.

Then, my aunt told me that Ruthie and the boyfriend had gotten engaged.

CHAPTER 10

'd always held Ruthie in high esteem. It was almost impossible not to, because my aunt absolutely adored her. Any ideas I had about dating Ruthie had always been countered by this thought: *I absolutely cannot date Ruthie for fun. Our families all know one another, and everyone will assume that our dating is serious.* I hadn't wanted to date Ruthie because I hadn't felt ready to be serious. But when I learned she'd gotten engaged, I sensed that I had missed an opportunity.

My aunt was ecstatic over Ruthie's engagement. To the contrary, Ruthie barely remembers anything about being engaged except that she got a lot of presents, including quite a few toaster ovens.

A couple of weeks later, she broke off the engagement and her relationship with the accountant boyfriend. Ruthie's father was devastated. He wanted to have a wedding celebration, a big affair. Her mother didn't react at all.

To this day, Ruthie says, "I remember returning the ring, but I don't remember much else."

Since Ruthie's mother and my aunt were best friends and spoke every night on the phone, my aunt was, of course, the first person to give me news of the breakup.

My response? I decided it was time for me to be serious and invited Ruthie out to dinner. I imagined she might be upset or need emotional support, and I knew she very well might not be interested in starting a relationship with me.

Ruthie, in her dating wisdom, did not even realize I was attempting to woo her. I thought it would be me and Ruthie alone at dinner, but she brought her best friend, Ronni, along with her.

As the three of us talked away at our table at Fiorello's, Ruthie excused herself to use the restroom. I asked Ronni, "So, how is she coping?"

"Coping? She doesn't even remember that she was engaged! She said to her mother, 'Return the gifts' and then hasn't spoken a word about it since."

That was an important lesson for me about Ruthie. When it comes to personal relationships, she tries very hard to make them work. But when one doesn't, she erases people from her memory, like hitting the delete button on a computer. For her, when it's over, it's over—feelings and all. All these years, I've behaved very well because I'm afraid of that delete button!

After our first "date" at Fiorello's, I called and asked for a second … and then a third and a fourth. We started seeing each other regularly for about two months. Today, when I ask Ruthie if by our second date she knew we were dating, she says, "Yeah, I think so." I tell people, "I am certain she knew that we were dating by the time I proposed to her."

In my memory of those first few dates, Ruthie was seeing me and another guy at the same time. After our second or third date, she told me as much, and I said to her, "Listen, *I* don't do that. You have to choose."

"I will take care of it" was all she said to me. She had deleted him by the next time I saw her.

And that was the start of our lifetime romance.

Now, you need to remember that I was still living in my uncle and aunt's basement. And you also need to know that I shared a car with my friend Mayer. A blue Chevy Impala. The two of us bought it together for $1,000.

The issue with the Impala was this: the car wouldn't start unless one of us jumped on the hood while the other pressed the ignition. Since we needed two of us to start the car, and since Mayer—for all the women he attracted—could also be quite lonely, he came along on all my dates with Ruthie that involved driving. Ruthie had her own car, a white Mustang with red upholstery, but she respectfully let me be the one to pick her up and drive us around. For the most part, the three of us would head out to a nearby diner, order blueberry cheesecake, and shuffle songs on the jukebox.

Just eight weeks into my relationship with Ruthie, I left to visit Israel for a month. When I met my parents at the airport, the first thing I did was tell them that I was getting married. To them, Ruthie was a jewel; my father was crazy about her, and my mother already loved her dearly. I was more than excited to share the news with them.

My mother's immediate reaction was "I have to go and call her mother!"

"You cannot call her mother," I instructed. "Ruthie doesn't know."

"What do you mean she doesn't know?"

"I didn't ask her yet. But I'm getting married."

"Are you sure she's going to say yes?"

"She'll say yes."

This conversation was repeated, nearly verbatim, with each visit I made to other family members, my friends, and even Ruthie's friends.

I told every one of them that we were getting married. And every one of them said, "I have to call her!" to which I answered, "You cannot call her!"

I was impressed that nobody called her. I was also impressed that most people treated my assertion as motivated by a great self-confidence (which is also the way I saw it) rather than derangement.

The night I got back from Israel, Ruthie came to see me at my aunt and uncle's place, and we sat together at the little round table in the kitchen. I had zero know-how when it came to asking someone to marry me. I didn't have a ring; I hadn't gone to her parents to tell them I wanted to get married. I just sat there, not knowing what to say but knowing that I intended to propose.

I leaned back in my chair and straight up asked Ruthie if she would like to marry me.

She said yes, at which point I leaned back just a little too far and fell to the ground.

When I recovered myself, I told Ruthie that everybody in Israel already knew about our engagement. She was shocked for about half a second and then laughed her head off.

When she went home and told her parents, they immediately phoned my aunt and uncle. I'll never forget lying in bed trying to fall asleep and then hearing two sets of footsteps—boom-boom-boom, boom-boom-boom-boom—charging down the stairs to the basement. The two of them burst into my room, and it took me a minute before I recognized what they were screaming and yelling about.

The very next day, there was a family party. Frankly, it seemed like a party every time we saw family, from the day we got engaged through to the day of our wedding. Everyone was beside themselves with joy and eager to celebrate. We would gather with relatives for

Friday dinner, and they would sing and dance around the table before we could sit down to eat.

Much later, Ruthie and I learned from her cousin Rhoda that some family members had reservations about our union or, at the very least, were "concerned." Ruthie had surprised everyone with her decisions—undertaken in such a short time span—both to end an engagement that made sense to everyone and then to commit to another engagement that people had a harder time understanding. I was not the person anyone had imagined Ruthie spending her life with. Ruthie was accomplished, driven, and brilliant; so far, I'd come to New York and rebuffed everyone's advice to go to Queens College and then made a commitment to having fun. Everyone wanted the absolute best for Ruthie; although I was tall, fit, and handsome (and confident!), the impression I gave was that I was a man who had not yet found a purpose or formed a plan for my life, let alone considered how to give shape to a life worthy of Ruthie's attention.

At the same time reservations were developing among some of Ruthie's family members, there was genuine obliviousness on her father's part. At that initial impromptu party, I learned that Leo hadn't even noticed that Ruthie and I were dating. A couple of weeks prior to our getting engaged, Leo had remarked offhandedly to Celia, "You know, Itzhak is spending a lot of time here lately." That had been his only recognition of anything developing between us. At the party, he pulled me aside and offered a teasing comment that drew on our different family histories in Poland and Lithuania, two countries united and divided over hundreds of years: "A Litvak!" he announced. "So be it."

I took his comment as the warmest of welcomes. It would be some time before I also understood it as a lesson in accepting what is, in letting life be.

When Celia pulled me aside that same evening, it was to gently inquire about Ruthie's and my plans for our wedding.

"When would you like to get married?" she asked.

"Next summer."

"Oh. *Why?*"

I had a good reason: "Well, my grandfather is old now, and there will have to be some planning to get him here from Israel." I was also looking forward to being engaged for a while, to fully enjoy the experience.

Ruthie's mother nodded and walked off, and I continued to mingle with the group.

Not fifteen minutes later, Celia came back around to me. "Your mother is on the phone, and she says they can come whenever the wedding is. No problem."

I could see that Ruthie's mother had applied her general rule: when you see something nice, you don't wait—you get it.

"Just let me know when I am getting married," I said with a smile, recognizing that I would not have much say when it came to the timing of our nuptials.

Our engagement was exactly three months long.

Ruthie and I were still finishing our degrees during the months leading up to our wedding. I decided to quit my job at EL AL and tried working for her father's optical goods business part time. Right off the bat, I made a great sale. At the time, Leo offered a few frames with heightened nose pads—these were not typical components of eyewear at the time. I visited a shop in Chinatown that placed a big order, and the owner became a lasting client of Leo's.

It was Ruthie's idea that I stop working for her father sooner rather than later. She didn't want me to feel obligated to participate in his business. But more than that, she wanted me to do my own thing, find my own way.

To solidify her point, she handed me the contact information for a job she'd seen posted on a bulletin board at NYU. The opening was for a teacher's assistant at an IBM training school.

My interviewer at IBM opened with the following remark: "New York Institute of Technology, eh? I thought we put ads at NYU."

"Eh," I answered, "NYIT is the MIT of New York."

The interviewer turned out to be a very warm person. He raised an eyebrow and then hired me on the spot.

My job was to teach the software and support students as they completed their assignments. I also developed familiarity with the IBM PC that had just come out. It was a big hit on the market, and the students were excited to learn how to use it.

Quitting my job at EL AL meant losing my diplomatic visa, and to start my employment at IBM, I needed a green card. So, Ruthie and I married civilly before our big religious wedding. The day before the civil ceremony, Ruthie had four wisdom teeth extracted. Her face was swollen and bruised; I couldn't help thinking that she looked as if I had beaten her. I noticed that the justice of the peace had absolutely no reaction.

Once we were civilly married, we got an apartment together on Fifty-Third Street and counted down the days until the big event.

In Israel, weddings are very informal. When my sister got married there, the whole event lasted less than an hour. In America, or at least in New York, weddings were, and still are, a much bigger deal.

I think about Ruthie's and my wedding as uniquely "one sided," by which I mean that everyone attending was already part of one big family. Often at weddings, you see two families coming together with people on either side meeting one another for the first time. But at our wedding, and given the long-standing relationships between our extended families, everyone was already united. That meant there was *a lot* of celebrating.

We married at the Sephardic Temple of Cedarhurst. The ceremony started at two in the afternoon on Thanksgiving Day, and the party didn't end until eleven at night. People went crazy for nine hours. Here were two families that had known each other forever, getting together to celebrate the continuation of life and an opportunity to build the next generation. Ruthie and I were also one of the first couples of the younger generation in America to wed, a fact that only contributed to the group's enthusiasm.

Three details of that day stand out to me even now.

The first is the ketubah signing, which has its own rituals involving the groom covering the bride's face prior to the more formal ceremony. That gesture signifies both the groom's love for the bride's inner beauty and that the two remain distinct individuals even after marriage.

Following tradition, I entered the room with all the men jumping and clapping and dancing in front of me, leading me to Ruthie for the bedecking, or veiling.

When they moved to the sides and I was finally standing in front of Ruthie, I looked first at her and then to my right and left and saw everybody crying. My mother was crying; all the neighbors from Queens were crying. I knew emotions were running high, and the joy they were experiencing in that room was haunted by the catastrophe they had survived not that long ago. Still, I was shocked to see all their tears.

What surprised me even more was that Ruthie was crying, too.

When I asked her, "Why are you crying?" she answered, "Because everybody else is crying!"

Ruthie jokes that prior to that moment, the last time anyone cried for me was after seeing my high school report cards. But that is untrue. My parents were not crying then. They were furious.

Second, my friend Doron made his first visit to America from Israel to celebrate with us. He also stayed in Ruthie's and my apartment for six weeks so that he could do some exploring before returning home. Another detail I remember is that the very minute the wedding ceremony ended, Doron—who is six foot four and a very strong guy—grabbed me, hoisted me onto his shoulders, and for an hour thereafter carried me around the room to greet all the guests.

The third detail is a noteworthy indicator of the thrill that circulated among both our families. My parents were so excited to come to the wedding that they took drugs—tranquilizers, to be exact. In no small dosage.

In every photo from that day, every movie clip featuring them, they look like total zombies, completely out of it, more than sufficiently numbed against the threat of too much happiness.

CHAPTER 11

As a wedding present, Leo bought me a Mazda RX-7. I'd wanted a sporty but not obnoxious two-seater, and I really liked the look of the hideaway headlights on the Mazda. One weekend not long after we were married, Ruthie's parents invited us to visit them in the Catskills. I had to work through the end of my shift on Friday before we could begin the drive. We took the Mazda and got caught up in a tremendous amount of traffic, so we didn't arrive to check into the hotel where her parents were staying until around midnight. We learned at the front desk that they no longer had a room ready for us.

Thinking nothing of it, we drove over to the motel just next door, checked in there, got some rest, and the next morning returned to the first hotel to meet up with Leo and Celia. What we had neglected to anticipate was their hysteria. Neither of them had slept. They imagined the reason we hadn't appeared on time was that we had gotten into a car accident and were dead. I assured them that the Mazda offered a safe and steady ride, but my sense was that it wouldn't have mattered if we'd driven there in a tank. I thought back to my parents overmedicating themselves to manage their joy at our wedding. Something similar was being expressed in Leo and Celia's hysteria—as if their happiness about our union and their wishes for our future were so intense that their fears and anxieties about losing us only increased.

If I'd discovered that day that Leo's capacity for worry was stronger than I'd imagined, soon thereafter I would learn that it was equally matched by his sense of discipline. Right after she finished law school, Ruthie had to study for the bar exam. She took a preparatory course from Pieper Bar Review and grew more and more anxious as the weeks went by. About halfway through the course, I picked her up from one of her classes, and she gave me a full speech about why she wasn't going to go through with finishing the course or taking the exam. She hadn't enjoyed law school to begin with, and the bar exam required way too much studying. She simply wasn't doing it.

I was a rookie at marriage, so I took her impassioned and anxious speech absolutely seriously. I called her father to have a conversation with him about how I should respond. "She doesn't want to do the bar," I began. I knew that wouldn't stop her from practicing law, but I also knew that it is always better to have passed the bar when you are working as an attorney.

Leo spoke the following words into the receiver: "She is going to study, she is going to take the exam, and she is going to pass." Then he hung up.

I might have guessed that's how our exchange would go. When it came to education, Leo's view was simple: you have to do it, and that's that.

I was surprised that Ruthie was so resistant to taking this final step in setting up her career, especially because she has a talent for figuring out and focusing on the most important things. People like me, on the other hand, have a lot less skill in differentiating between more important and less important details. We will read the whole book sentence by sentence, cover to cover, without a strong sense of where to put our attention instead of keying in on the primary messages and most salient points.

Ruthie passed the bar, and she's been practicing law without wanting to practice law for more than forty years now.

What she did right after the exam, however, was start taking classes at NYU toward earning an MBA. During Ruthie's first year in business school, we also had our first child.

I've mentioned that second-generation Holocaust survivors inherited the insanity of their parents when it comes to enthusiasm for their children. Our kids mean everything to us because the continuation of the family has, for us, the additional significance of feeling like we are winning against those who tried to destroy our people. From the moment *we* were born, we were miracle children. Our parents were not supposed to live; then they had us. So, for us, taking that next step forward by having children of our own has an added significance. Our kids are everything. They always will be.

Me? I was crazy about having boys. My father had two brothers and one sister who survived. Of his two brothers, David had two daughters, and Eliezer had two daughters and the one son, Gidon, who died serving in the Israeli army. That meant that on the Fisher side, I was the only one left who could pass on the family name—thus the importance I placed on having a son.

That said, Ruthie is the one who decided when we were going to have children. She is also the one who decided that we would *not* consider moving to Israel until some time had passed after our first child was born. We had agreed that at some point we would try living in Israel, and given that she was close with her parents, Ruthie wanted them to enjoy having a grandchild at least for a little while before we left the US.

Ruthie's doctor was amazing. He had earned quite a reputation for never having missed a delivery over the course of his entire career. Little did he know that Ruthie would put that record to the test. She was in labor for over thirty-five hours before our first son, Gidon—named after my cousin—was born. Over the course of those thirty-five hours, we drove to the hospital four times, each time believing that Ruthie was ready to be admitted.

They finally did admit her around the thirtieth hour, and five hours after that, Ruthie recognized that she was giving birth and called out, "It's time!" Ruthie's nurse and I were in the room with her, watching a Yankees game on the television. After all the hours Ruthie had been in labor, when she finally did call out, I heard myself call back, "Wait, wait, wait. It's the ninth inning, there are two outs, and there are just a couple of minutes left!"

Ruthie had to repeat herself in order to divert both my and the nurse's attention: "*It's tiiiime!*" she called out again.

Of course, when Gidi was born, I was insane. He had a long face and looked totally beaten up, but what I saw was the best-looking kid in the nursery. All the nurses kindly agreed with me when I ran around telling people that my son was the best-looking guy there.

Ruthie always needs to have some larger purpose or project on which she's working—and an office to go to. So, not long after Gidi was born, she started working for a firm that had about eight partners and was … well, an interesting place. Her boss's boss, one of the senior partners, was a Harvard grad who was drunk most of the day. But Ruthie enjoyed working for her direct boss and stayed at that firm for about two years doing general corporate law.

After two years at IBM, I was approached by a headhunter who offered me an opportunity to consult for Mobil Oil. I would oversee the implementation of software and personal computers within the company. It was 1982, I was twenty-six years old, and the salary they offered me was a crazy $250,000. Far more successful people twice my age were not making that much money. I took the job and also decided to start earning a master of computer science degree at NYU.

Toward the end of my second year of consulting at Mobil Oil, I got bored. Not much work was left to do introducing the IBM PC to all the executives, but the organization was such that I could have stayed around and done nothing for another year, maybe more. That's when Ruthie and I decided that we should go to Israel. So, when the company asked, "How much more time do you need to continue your consultation here?" I shocked them a bit with my answer: "I'm going to leave at the end of the year, because my family and I are moving."

I'd met the person charged with starting a company for a big Israeli conglomerate that at the time owned the Israeli Yellow Pages telephone business directory. That company decided that electronic mail—a service you had to pay for back then—was going to replace telex machines, which transmitted typed messages over dedicated telephone lines. (By the way, email eventually did replace the telex, but not before telex was directly replaced by fax machines.)

I became employee number two at the start-up, which was named Aurec Goldnet.

Looking back on it now, I would say that when Ruthie and I married, I was pretty immature. I think she may even have thought that about me, but she also has a tremendous capacity for believing in me. And since she's a very tolerant person, she went along with a lot of my nonsense while I found my way. Here I was, choosing to leave an easy consulting gig so I could try out being a salaried employee in an Israeli start-up, earning something like $36,000 a year—about a seventh of my salary in the US. When I left Mobil Oil and ventured into the Aurec start-up environment, neither of us knew that there would be many years and many risky moves before I finally discovered my true talents and started putting them to good use.

And though she wanted to try raising a family in Israel, moving there was no small risk for Ruthie, either. Her prior experience living in Israel hadn't gone well—she'd felt isolated from friends and family both physically and emotionally—and I knew she'd need a job and a purpose to keep her from having a meltdown at the idea of being a homemaker. We were twenty-eight, just starting a family, and taking a risk that would have economic, professional, social, and emotional consequences.

To other people, Ruthie and I may have seemed to be very different from each other, but I've always thought that our deep bond was the product of all that we had in common right from the start. When we got together, people would ask her how she could marry an Israeli, given that we'd grown up worlds apart. "But we have such great similarities!" she'd answer, unable to understand how people couldn't see what was so obvious. When people pointed out to her that I didn't have much of a career plan, Ruthie would answer, "He'll figure it out," and leave it at that. For Ruthie, it was natural to date and marry an Israeli as well as someone who hadn't ever imagined himself becoming a doctor, a lawyer, or an accountant. For me, it was natural to fall in love with a brilliant and independent woman from New York whose patience grounded me.

Before we married, I would occasionally say to Ruthie, "Eventually I want to go back to Israel and live there."

And she would say, "Of course."

She never lost the desire to have a life in Israel, so there were no debates, no big conversations. For both of us, it was very clear that we would take that step and then see what followed.

Unfortunately, Ruthie's mother did not share that same attitude. Whereas Leo responded to the news about Aurec by encouraging us to go to Israel and live our lives, Celia did not take well to the fact that we were moving far away—more specifically, she did not take well to the fact that reliable, responsible, and grounded Ruthie would be moving away from her home in New York.

CHAPTER 12

We had a soft landing in Israel because my family was there and Ruthie already spoke the language. My parents rented us an apartment before we arrived, and we stayed in that place for a couple of years before buying an apartment in a new building as it was just being finished.

At Aurec, I wanted to start selling right away, so one of the first things we did was sit with the company lawyer to create a customer contract. The lawyer's first draft document had a clause that said something like, "If we sold you email and you are not paying the bill, we can come to your office and take your mailbox away." That's how new the concept of an electronic mailbox was in Israel. For a company that was ahead of its time, Aurec did pretty well.

As head of marketing and sales, I got my first taste of supervisory work. I learned how to manage sales, how to position product, and how to hire well. But all that learning was not without some distress. To this day, I can recall being told by the company's owner, just after I landed that first big deal, that I needed to fire someone. When I asked, "Why on earth would I do that?" the owner replied, "So everyone knows there's accountability within this organization."

I made sense of the seemingly arbitrary directive by deciding to fire the lowest-performing salesperson. I didn't sleep at all the night before I had to call this man into my office and let him go, and by the time our conversation took place, I was literally shaking. I can say now that it was not my best professional moment, but I did keep up a relationship with the man after firing him and even recommended him for other work.

To help us establish a community outside work, Ruthie suggested that I volunteer for Benjamin Netanyahu's campaign for parliament. Bibi was the Israeli UN ambassador before running for an elected office, and people already thought of him as a rising political star. I became part of Bibi's advisory group—"the submarine" was that group's name—and we all met once a week to discuss and agree on campaign strategy and plans. One of the more ingenious things Bibi's team did to work around campaign finance rules was spend early donations (those received prior to the campaign start date) on voter-registration kiosks. The kiosks, located primarily in shopping malls, registered people to the Likud party—so that they could then also vote for Bibi. Those kiosks added another hundred thousand voters to the party.

At the first meeting of the submarine, Bibi gave us volunteers official roles. Mine was campaign treasurer. It was a role I didn't necessarily feel qualified to do, but I did balance the campaign budget, and that accomplishment earned Bibi a reputation for being a clean politician.

Bibi won a position in parliament, and in a later campaign, when he became head of the Likud party, he made me the party's treasurer—a role I fulfilled for two years in the early 1990s. In that role, and by reviewing municipal elections in Israel, I was able to get the party out of $10 million in debt. That's also when I learned that I was the very first party treasurer to use an Excel spreadsheet and the first to run a balanced budget!

My engagement in politics was both a once-in-a-lifetime experience and one that I had no desire to continue. I appreciated that it gave me a new perspective on Israeli affairs along with access to high-level decision-makers, but I couldn't see myself getting any more deeply involved than that. I could see just how much corruptive influence came along with increasing power. I had no trouble imagining the ease with which lives could be ruined.

That said, we did do some interesting things during the general election. Ronald Reagan loved the Likud party and sent his personal pollster Dick Wirthlin to help us. Wirthlin brought with him a young guy named Frank Luntz. I had taken leave from Aurec to help with the election, and the two of them worked with me for that three-month period. Together, we introduced three systems that were new to Israel at that time. One of them was flash polling. Immediately after our political commercials aired, our team would call voters for their impressions in order to measure the efficacy of campaign advertising. Another was the use of focus groups. We invited undecided voters to watch commercials and respond in real time by pushing a series of buttons indicating what effect our advertisements had on them. And the third system was statistical analysis. Our effort may have been the first time anywhere in the world that statistics from previous elections were mapped by residential area alongside details like average income and education. We color-coded maps of areas all over Israel and then distributed those maps to all the activists in the Likud party for use in targeting our base.

The polling systems were successful—for the most part. The young Frank, who had been put in charge of one of the key strategic systems, learned a couple of things about Israelis during his visit. First, he learned that if you presented data the politicians liked, everything went well; if you presented data they didn't like, you were likely to be outright challenged or dismissed with an "Eh, what the hell are you talking about!?"

Second, on the night before the election, I accompanied Frank on a visit to then–prime minister Yitzhak Shamir. Frank proudly conveyed all his data, telling Shamir in no uncertain terms, "Tomorrow, you are losing the election." Shamir did not lose the election, and Frank discovered that when you ask people in Israel about their voting plans, many of them lie.

That was a traumatic experience for Frank, and it took him years to recover. Thankfully, during the months that he was living in a hotel in Israel, he would come over to our apartment for dinner. Ruthie would feed him schnitzel and rice, and then he would relax by playing Nintendo with six-year-old Gidi. And I got to have a unique experience postelection when Wirthlin introduced the statistical analysis piece of our work to the Tories in England; I went there for a couple of weeks to help them implement the same systems we used.

I had taken a three-month hiatus from work to help with the Likud general election campaign, but once that was through, I returned to Aurec. I continued on as treasurer of the Likud party and stayed at Aurec for another three years—totaling seven overall—before I felt it was time for me to move on. I stayed that long at Aurec largely because that company did genius-level work on employee retention. In addition to a whole host of other perks, once a year all the employees and their families were treated to a vacation together. The company also sponsored employee participation in sports leagues. I played basketball and soccer, and in basketball, our team won the league championship. Believe it or not, there were even Olympic games for our leagues. I traveled to former Yugoslavia one year to participate in those.

Aurec was such a family-friendly environment that I found it difficult to leave even when the company was not doing very well. Toward the end of my employment there, the board decided to fire the CEO and offered me his job. I knew the company inside and out, but I didn't see a way to make it profitable in the short term. The board didn't like my approach because it wanted profitability, so they ended up hiring someone else. I had been a strong second-in-charge and partner to the CEO, who had started the company. I always said exactly what I thought, and he'd appreciated just that. But when the new CEO came on board, I could see that my habit of voicing my opinions wasn't aligned with his methods.

Once that dynamic changed, leaving became easy.

Having political connections ended up serving me well, especially when it came time for me to exit Aurec. Even though I had decided to quit my job and see what I could do on my own, I wanted to be sure I received the compensation that was in my contract. Because I'd quit, I shouldn't have received any compensation, but the organization recognized that I was very well connected politically and invited me to sit down with the CFO of the whole conglomerate to negotiate.

"What would you like?" he asked.

I outlined what was in my contract: "Well, it says I should get this, and this ..."

"How much money is that in total?"

"I think it's this and this ..."

"Okay, you can have it."

You never know until you ask, I thought to myself at the close of that conversation. And when you're well connected, it's always good to ask.

CHAPTER 13

At Aurec, I was able to connect Celia and Ruthie via email. At first, Celia refused to write messages, but eventually the two of them started writing to each other every night and settled into an arrangement to visit four times each year, each one making two trips to see the other.

Ruthie took the bar exam in Israel, and for the first two years that we lived there, she worked in the legal department of a bank, only to learn that it was not for her. Among other things, the atmosphere was highly political. She'd been hired as an English-speaking attorney, but there was very little work for her to do. She was bored most days, and the British fellows who worked there wouldn't share their work with her—it was, after all, their means of proving their worth to the bank.

When the bank hired two law students from Harvard and handed them off to work with Ruthie for the summer, she didn't know what to do with them. The three of them completed a single project together, and then she sent them out on field trips to visit historical sites that had nothing to do with the law. They went out, learned things, had a good time doing it, and then turned in reports to Ruthie about what they had discovered.

When the summer ended and the law students left, Ruthie decided to go to the head of the legal department and ask for more work. She was probably the first lawyer in the entire history of the bank to do this, and she made the mistake of asking more than once.

In Israel at that time, if you worked for a bank and there was nothing for you to do, then there was nothing for you to do. Twice a day at Ruthie's bank, an older woman pushed around a cart offering tea and cakes. It was the highlight of everyone's day—for some, choosing a pastry was the most effort they put into their work hours. Ruthie tried to learn the ways of the office; she even started going home for a spell in the middle of the workday to complete some house chores. Ruthie would nap on the bus, do a load of laundry or some other task at home, and then take the bus back to the office. Nobody at the office ever noticed.

But she'd had the audacity to ask for more work. So, of course, she was fired.

By then, we had our second son, Ron. While newly pregnant, Ruthie had taken Gidi to New York for Passover, and during a routine checkup there, her doctor discovered a medical issue that needed addressing. She needed major surgery, so instead of coming back to Israel, she stayed at her parents' house in Great Neck for about six months of her pregnancy. I started traveling to New York every month so that we could all spend time together.

With Gidi, you'll recall, we visited the hospital multiple times over a period of thirty-five hours. With Ron, we were sitting in bed at her parents' house in Great Neck, and when I turned to Ruthie to say that I was going to sleep, she said calmly, "I don't think it's a good idea for you to sleep. I think I'm having the baby." She'd been in labor for a few hours already but had waited to say anything until her contractions were about thirty seconds apart! I leaped out of bed, loaded our things into the car, and drove like a maniac into the city. We ran into the hospital, where they took one look at Ruthie and brought her straight to the delivery room. A half hour later, there was a baby. True to his record, our doctor—the same doctor who had delivered Gidi a couple of years earlier—came rushing into the delivery room, pushed aside the doctor who was there on call, and delivered our second son.

On this second visit to the hospital, I noticed they had started offering patients televisions and telephones in their rooms. In Israel, we had nothing of the sort. As it turned out, one of Ruthie's cousins, Ricky, owned one of the businesses that provided those services, so before we left, I talked with him about the possibility of doing something similar in Israel.

When we returned to Tel Aviv, I figured Ruthie could use a change in her work, so I helped her get a job with the number one PR office in all Israel. And she liked it! She worked with some very nice people, and she had a good task: representing Israeli companies to foreign journalists. At the time, not a lot of firms were focusing effort on foreign journalists, so she had a good angle to pursue and met a lot of interesting people. Nearly every country had a correspondents' office in Israel, and pretty much anyone reporting on the Middle East was stationed there. Not every day was a big news day, so those correspondents had time on their hands and space in their papers to report on other things. Ruthie would meet with them and suggest stories they might pursue. Any time they wrote about one of the PR firm's companies, that was a big win for her.

Through that office, she came to know a fellow with a PhD in strategic studies who wrote for *Jane's Defence Weekly*, a very well-respected publication. He'd been writing content for *Jane's* for some time but needed to step away from that work and focus on other responsibilities. So, he invited Ruthie to start working as a journalist and writing in collaboration with him, and he eventually gave her all his leads and relationships with news outlets.

In Israel, everything is defense. Writing about defense is nearly the same as writing about politics in general. As *Jane's* correspondent in Israel, Ruthie would talk to heads of the military industry at press conferences; she would meet generals, ministers, and other higher-ups. And because of my access to people in government, she could bring her editors from London and Washington, DC, to meet and interview nearly whomever they wanted.

At one point, I arranged for her to meet and interview the defense minister of Israel, who at that time had just come into his role. His English was awful, so Ruthie tried speaking to him in Hebrew. But he insisted on answering her in English, even though the words he strung together made no sense whatsoever.

The minister's spokesman was shaking during the interview, because he knew it was a disaster. As Ruthie tells it, the spokesman walked her out of the room and said something like, "What are we going to do with this?" Ruthie told the spokesman not to worry. She went home and wrote entirely new answers to the questions she'd posed. When the spokesman and the rest of the minister's team saw the interview Ruthie had written up, they called to tell her how much they loved her. From that point forward, she would get invited to meet with them, attend events—she had whatever access they were able to offer.

The funny thing is that the minister seemed fascinated by his English-language answers, almost as if he believed that what Ruthie had written was, in fact, exactly what he'd said to her.

While Ruthie was discovering the full range of her journalistic talents, I was learning what it was like to start my own business. When

I quit Aurec, it was because I'd found a partner willing to go in with me on the plan to put televisions and telephones into Israeli hospital rooms. I should say that I'm not a hospital guy; I walk into any facility and immediately feel sick. So, I created a bit of a challenge for myself by coming up with a business idea requiring my office to be located inside a hospital. On the first day I was supposed to report there, I actually drove to the Aurec offices instead—and I don't think that was just a matter of habit.

Our little company signed agreements with eleven hospitals, all for between ten and fifteen years of rental service. In my opinion, we were geniuses for putting in a clause that mimicked the electronic-mailbox mistake the Aurec lawyers had made in their first draft: if a hospital were to end its contract with us short of the agreed-upon time frame, we retained the right to pull all the wires out of the walls.

What Ruthie remembers about those two years is the attitude of the people around us toward my decision to leave Aurec—and the salary it provided—so that I could try working independently. We had a lot of friends and family members whose wives were hovering over their husbands' careers and telling them what to do. Ruthie was very cool when it came to all my decisions.

"How can you let your husband not have a salary?" they would wonder aloud to her. "Why doesn't he have a real profession?"

"It will be fine," she'd answer. "We're going to be fine."

Honestly, I think what annoyed her more than their "concern" for my career was their view of why my business partner Smulik and I took a trip to Club Med in the Alps so that I could learn to ski. Ruthie's women friends called to tell her she was completely crazy to let me go on a trip that would give me the opportunity to cheat on her.

I remember listening to Ruthie say into the telephone, "I don't know where you grew up, but everybody I know who ever cheated on their spouses cheated right in the same city where they lived. They didn't have to go all the way to Club Med to do that!"

I felt proud in that moment ... then much less so when I discovered just how difficult and exhausting it is learning to ski. I remember coming back to the hotel room one afternoon, throwing myself on the bed, and yelling to Smulik, "Get me a cinnamon roll and a glass of water!" When he did, I couldn't even lift myself up to drink from the glass. But I kept learning, and now every year I take our sons, their cousins, and their friends on a big ski trip—just the guys.

What I remember most about those couple of years is that Ruthie decided to use the money she had been saving in her own personal account to buy all new furniture for our living room. She purchased a very fancy black couch and two mustard-yellow chairs, and on the day they were delivered and set up in our space, she decided that she hated them. For weeks, she refused to enter that room, and when she had to sit in an adjacent room, she'd drape a kitchen towel over the side of her head to avoid catching sight of it. For weeks, I had to look at her wearing a towel over her head. A month later, she finally asked a neighbor to have a look at what she'd bought, and the neighbor was enthusiastic: "These look really good!" Thankfully, Ruthie decided soon after that she liked the couch and chairs enough to return the kitchen towel to its more useful place.

The two years I worked on the hospital project was also a very interesting period politically in Israel. The first Gulf War occurred in 1991. Missiles were flying overhead, everyone was calling to check on family and friends, and the telecommunications infrastructure was challenged to the point of collapse.

What stands out to me most when I look back on that period is that Ruthie's father came to visit only a week before the official start of the war. Here we all were, acquiring gas masks, boarding up windows, and preparing shelters, and there was Leo, landing in Tel Aviv cool as a cucumber, ready to do the things he usually does on a trip to Israel: visit family, visit the bank, visit the cemetery. He did all his things, had a great time, boarded the plane back to the US, and just three days after he left, the missiles started dropping. I suppose that as a Holocaust survivor, he'd already seen the worst. A little war in Israel wasn't going to faze him one bit.

Ruthie's and my experience of the war was a bit different from Leo's. When we returned to Israel and I reentered the reserves—and because my file contained that letter from the head of the navy—I had been able to stay with the navy for my initial assignments. But my reserve duty guarding the port in Haifa was really boring. So, I reached out to a couple of friends and, given my training, matched with a unit that taught soldiers how to use computers. I did that for a couple of years before getting bored again, and that time around, my connections helped me get into the military spokesperson unit. For the most part, being in that unit involved showing off the bases and the soldiers to wealthy or famous people. When hairstylist and businessman Vidal Sassoon visited, I took him to see the air force base, where he donated a club for the soldiers.

But when war broke out, I was assigned to Jerusalem to give briefings for foreign journalists. Our next-door neighbor in Tel Aviv had taken the whole situation quite seriously and nailed mattresses up against the windows and hung gas masks from the mattresses for easy access. Ruthie and I were not as vigilant, even though that war was our first experience seeing missiles directly overhead and witnessing the use of gas masks. What we did instead—and given that I would be away in Jerusalem for six weeks—was decide that my parents should live with Ruthie and the boys.

What stands out about the rest of that experience is that timely information about the war was often more accessible to people outside the country than in it. Not always, mind you, as on the occasion when one of my duties was to speak with Ted Koppel on *Nightline* along with Natan Sharansky and an American woman who had immigrated to Israel. When Koppel asked me, "Will there be a war with Israel?" I answered, "Yes, and that's not a bad thing. We need to get rid of a dictator once and for all." It was funny to me when Koppel insisted that I was mistaken, citing his own recent conversation with the king of Jordan as evidence—that there would be no war.

The war with Israel broke out the night after that interview, and from that point forward, all the most up-to-date information came to us from CNN. CNN reported the firing of missiles before any Israeli authority knew, and Ruthie's and my US friends were the ones calling us directly to tell us, well before any alarms went off, that missiles were headed toward the country. The one advantage I had in my role was that I could call and tell Ruthie exactly where the missiles had fallen, alleviating for the most part any worry she or my parents might have about the rockets' nearness to our family home.

There were a few very serious moments during the war when we headed north for a couple of days to stay with my uncle's family on the kibbutz or to stay with Zipi and her family, but in the end, Ruthie, the kids, and my parents all had a wonderful time living together. The kids had lots of playtime with friends. They all ate great meals cooked by my mother. The apartment was open to many visitors, and Ruthie and my father bonded by watching television and drinking beer together each night. At the end of the war, my father was very upset that he and my mother were going to have to stop living with us.

Because of my role in the defense spokesperson unit, I met and established a relationship with the CEO of a company called Bezeq, a major Israeli telecommunications service provider. The CEO, Itzhak Kaul, was an amazing guy and a total workaholic. He'd headed a very strong union, headed HR for Bezeq, and then moved into the CEO position at the Israel Postal Authority and really transformed that organization from a laughingstock into something respectable. When he was asked to return to Bezeq as its CEO, he invited me to join him as a consultant.

I sold my portion of the hospital operation to Smulik and went with Itzhak to every meeting and did all of his PR. Not only did I learn about the telecom industry; I also kept learning how to work with journalists. The only downside was that I would leave home at seven in the morning and not return until midnight, six days a week.

When I joined Bezeq, in Israel people were still waiting eight or nine years to get a home telephone line. My own parents waited that long. But Itzhak changed all that. He started advertising that people could place an order online and get their phones within a week.

Of course, the entire country chose Bezeq, and this is why we were so busy all the time. Itzhak was excellent at treating workers well. He was very aware that he was asking them to work evenings, weekends—basically around the clock—to ensure that the company lived up to its promise. He would take me with him to a site, bring the workers whiskey, and spend time checking in on them professionally and personally.

To resolve important issues that arose each week, we would have team meetings that started on Thursdays at four in the afternoon and didn't end until after midnight. People were tormented by the sheer length of those meetings. After a while, I discovered that Itzhak was obsessed with press releases. So, to distract him for a bit—and give everyone a break for twenty minutes or so—I would bring to the meeting the week's press about the company and about him as its leader. Everyone enjoyed the twenty minutes of quiet as Itzhak focused all his attention on the press clippings.

After two years of consulting at Bezeq, I couldn't take the long hours anymore. Thankfully, by then I'd received a job offer to start a company that would compete with Bezeq, but only on its data and fax services. The new company, called ClalCom, was being started by Clal Industries—the largest conglomerate in Israel. Another guy and I were hired as co-CEOs. That was a smart move on Clal's part, because my co-CEO had been the representative to Sprint Corporation at the company he was hired away from, and from my work at Bezeq, I had developed a strong relationship with AT&T.

My time at ClalCom was short lived, and my sole memory is of a bid we lost to be a second operator of cellular phones in Israel. What I remember most is not that we lost the license but that I collected some data during the process, and our team couldn't believe the numbers: Israel was number one in the world for people talking on the phone for long lengths of time. What can I say? When we talk, we talk.

When I decided that I wasn't excited about working at ClalCom anymore, I came home and told Ruthie, "I have to find myself. I need to see what else I can do working on my own." I had a lot of anxiety about what that decision would mean when it came to cash flow for the family. But I wanted to be independent and knew that I had to follow my inclination.

"Do what you need to do" was her calm response.

I didn't quit ClalCom flat out. First, I went to the owner and told him that 1 percent ownership in the company didn't have an upside for me. He asked, "How much do you want?"

"Ten percent," I answered.

He didn't say anything in the moment, and he didn't say anything for a full three months afterward. So, at the three-month mark, I went back to him to initiate the same conversation.

That's when I realized I would not get the 10 percent. And *that's* when I quit.

During that same period—for about two years leading up to my quitting—Ruthie and I had been going through the agonizing experience of fertility treatments to have another child. We thought our kids were marvelous, so of course we wanted another one. Over the course of eleven IVF procedures, we tried to grow our family. Though the doctor was exceptionally nice and took good care of Ruthie, it did not help at all that he started out by saying that Ruthie was an easy case. And though socialized medicine made it possible for us to try as many times as we did, it was in no way easy going through that process in Israel, where everyone was thoroughly obsessed with childbearing.

People had already started to comment that there would be a five-year gap between our youngest son and a new baby. It wasn't just friends who offered unsolicited comments; everywhere Ruthie went, strangers would approach with their questions: "How many children do you have? Only two boys? What if they are killed in the army? God forbid something should happen to them. You should have more children. You should try to have a girl. They are better overall. They will go shopping with you, and they are the ones who will take care of you when you are old." I remembered my own grandfather saying to my mother that her purpose was to take care of her parents. It's an assumption in the culture and one that my mother resented deeply.

My way of dealing with all those comments was to point out how many times Ruthie tried to get pregnant. But Ruthie didn't feel she had to explain herself to people, not even when the boys were right there to witness the awkwardness. One day, the three of them were approached in a shopping center by a woman we barely knew.

"Oh," she said, furrowing her brow and pointing at the boys, "Is this all you have?"

Gidi was old enough at the time to notice that the woman's comment didn't seem particularly nice. He looked up at Ruthie from the lime-green scooter he took with him everywhere and asked, "What did she mean, we are all you have?" Ruthie remembers telling Gidi that the woman was just so very impressed with them both. She left it at that, hoping that if she didn't give the encounter any more attention, perhaps neither would Gidi.

The straw that broke the camel's back, so to speak, occurred when Ruthie was out with our youngest son, Ron. They ran into the father-in-law of one of our good friends. This man had seen us at two or three events over the entirety of the time we'd lived in Israel. But that didn't stop him from approaching Ruthie to say, "You know, you are very lazy when it comes to having kids." She was too stunned to say anything in response. That wasn't the first time an Israeli man had attributed our small family size to Ruthie being lazy. The word had stuck with her. But after hearing it repeated on this occasion, and after getting her hopes up eleven times, she decided she'd had enough. The eleventh try was our last.

By the time I quit ClalCom and she quit IVF attempts, we were both depleted and exhausted. Ruthie never said how miserable she was dealing with all that external pressure, but I could see that she was depressed. She put no pressure on me at the time, never asked to move back to New York. But the way she describes that period now, she knew that I was looking for a way to save her.

ClalCom represented Sprint, and right around the time I quit my job there, Sprint offered me a first-class ticket to that year's World

Cup in the US. I traveled along with the CEO of Bezeq, who had been my boss only a short time earlier. One of two things was true for me during the entirety of that trip: either people treated me nicely because I was traveling with the CEO of Bezeq, or people treated me nicely because they believed *I* was the CEO of Bezeq. When I left for that trip, I asked Bibi to connect me with Ronald Lauder, the younger son of Estée Lauder—founder of the famous cosmetics and fragrance company—and himself an incredibly active philanthropist and businessman.

On my way back home, I stopped in New York to have a conversation with Ronald. I might have worried about our family's economic situation and Ruthie's well-being, but I never worried about having a business idea. I came up with a proposition for him the day before we were scheduled to talk. I had no presentation to give, just an idea about which I spoke extemporaneously.

My idea, born in part from that bit of research I did while at ClalCom, was to reduce the cost of international telephone calls. At the time, a telephone monopoly existed in most countries in the world, and deregulation was just getting underway. I saw this as an opportunity to intervene in the international call market.

Ronald received my idea warmly. "How much money do you have?" he asked me.

"If you turn me upside down and shake me, you'll see that I have about four hundred thousand dollars," I answered.

"You put in your four hundred thousand, and I will contribute the rest of what you need to start the company. We will be fifty-fifty owners, and you will work here alongside me in New York."

The offer was generous, and I did not allow myself to take it seriously. My idea was just that—an idea. As yet, I had no business plan. Besides that, I'd learned from Bibi and others that Ronald's enthusiasm for business ventures did not necessarily lead to deals. Though Ronald promised he would come to Israel, arrange a meeting of our lawyers, and formalize the plan, I felt I had good reason to be cautious. I also did not want to discuss the opportunity with Ruthie unless Ronald and I actually reached an agreement. There was no way I was going to give her false hope about moving home to New York. Imagine my surprise when Ronald and I ran into one another in the lobby of a Hilton hotel in Tel Aviv only a week later, wrote the primary points of our deal on a napkin, and signed an agreement that I would invest my $400,000, he would invest $5 million, I would own 34 percent of the company, and he would own the rest!

I'd just taken a big risk from which I hoped would eventually come a big reward. I put the entirety of our savings into a start-up company and initiated a plan that would move us back across the Atlantic to a place the boys had only ever visited. We were leaving family and friends in Tel Aviv, and we would have to make the move relatively quickly.

Ruthie and I joke now about how, when the business opportunity in America came up, she eagerly packed just two suitcases and announced that she was ready to go. She could not take being in Israel anymore.

Within two weeks after Ronald and I signed our names to a cocktail napkin, Ruthie, the boys, and I moved to Manhattan to begin a new life there.

CHAPTER 14

Back in 1984, when we moved to Tel Aviv, Gidi was just a year and a half old. Ron was born four years later, and then it wasn't until 1994—when the boys were eleven and seven—that we returned to the US. In Ron's earliest months, he acquired the nickname "Chooby."

"He just looks like a Chooby," Gidi commented one day, studying Ron's round, smiling face.

Not only did we start calling him Chooby at home; everyone around us agreed that this was a most appropriate nickname for him. Even our pediatrician said, "I don't know what it means, but it really suits him!"

Ron himself liked the name so much that he's been responsible for carrying it forward into his adult life.

When it came to raising children, Israel at that time was very different from the US. In Israel, where the whole world essentially revolves around children, you send your kids out of the house to roam free, firmly believing that they are eminently safe. In America, at least in New York at that time, you didn't let your kids out of your sight. We felt lucky that our boys were able to spend some of their youth with that easy freedom and independence.

Gidi was a very social guy growing up in Tel Aviv; he had lots of friends throughout elementary school and was crazy into sports. For the most part, he was a very good kid, only occasionally and mildly and comically "disruptive"—like when, at age six, he decided to run away from home. He packed his little backpack, stood at the door, and announced to Ruthie, "I don't want to be here anymore. I'm leaving you." She can't recall what made him so adamant about running off, but she calmly replied, "Okay, goodbye," and watched as he got into the elevator of our apartment building. Ten minutes later, Ruthie buzzed the intercom in the lobby and said, "Gidi, come home for dinner." Having already grown bored sitting on a lobby bench, Gidi issued a begrudging "Oh-kaaay," and dutifully came back upstairs.

While Gidi was exploring the limits of his freedom, Chooby was already developing his entrepreneurial capacities. At age four, he decided he needed to make some money to buy lunch for himself and his best friend. When I arrived home from work one afternoon, a neighbor got into the elevator with me and said, "Your son sold me bananas today." I learned that Chooby had taken some of the produce out of our refrigerator, set a price for each item, and gone door to door peddling his goods. He couldn't yet write the words, so he showed potential customers a menu of offerings: his hand-drawn pictures of each fruit or vegetable with the going price listed beneath. Numbers he could do. At each door, he proffered his list—and quite a few neighbors bought something from him.

Chooby and his friend got their pizza and colas for lunch, and from the experience Chooby drew a conclusion that he's also taken with him into adult life: "I told you," he announced to his friend that afternoon, "it's so easy to make money!"

We moved to the US right when Gidi was about to shift from elementary to junior high school, and in all honesty, we told the boys and everyone else that we were going to try living in the States for one year while I worked on starting up a business. Gidi was not necessarily happy about the move, but he adjusted within about a week's time. I suspect that the tentativeness of our commitment to living in New York helped ease the transition for him. He'd already spent summers in the US; he could tell his friends in Israel that he was likely to be back in a year; and on this trip, we brought one of his good friends to spend the summer with us in New York. Gidi had the additional advantage of making new friends in New York at just about the time in their lives when they were acquiring more freedom to move about unsupervised. They took the public bus to school, they went with their friends to do homework at the local bookstore, and they went out for ice cream in the neighborhood. Also, they were at the age when all the bat and bar mitzvah parties started happening, which provided them all with perfect entertainment. In those initial couple of years, there were so many bar and bat mitzvahs that Gidi thought it was totally normal to go to a fancy party every weekend.

When we first told Ruthie's parents about the move back to the US, Leo insisted that we live with him and Celia in Great Neck. We did stay with them for a little while, while we looked for a place to live. Initially, I went back to Israel to close on the apartment there, and Ruthie took charge of finding our new home. At the time, there weren't any online databases featuring available inventory like there are now, so she started out by stalking apartment complexes she liked in the Upper West Side. She would go from doorman to doorman inquiring about availability. When she looked at the building in which we currently live, she was able to talk with the broker there, who told Ruthie that one apartment was available for rent but that another couple was already in the process of renting it. He probably shouldn't have, but he let Ruthie see the apartment. Ruthie was thankful for that—on seeing the place, she knew immediately that she wanted it for our family.

Two days after the broker showed her the apartment, she visited a coffee shop across the street that gave her a clear view of his office. When she noticed that he was just sitting at his desk, she crossed the street and entered the building to talk with him.

"Who are you?" he asked when she knocked on his door.

"I was just here talking with you the other day!" she replied.

"Oh, right. Come back on Monday."

We did, and he offered us the apartment on the spot.

We sent Gidi to a Jewish day school called Heschel whose curriculum had a perfect balance of tradition and religion. Actually, we tried to send both Gidi and Chooby to the same school, but they had very different interview experiences. Gidi was anxious but then walked into the administrator's office and had a fabulous interview. Chooby, on the other hand ... we heard from the interviewers that though Chooby was very bright, he was also all over the place, literally wandering around the room, rearranging papers on the interviewer's desk, occasionally climbing up onto the desk—and whenever he was asked a question, he would respond by posing his own questions in return.

He did not get accepted there.

Both boys could speak English well, but neither of them could read or write in the language at grade level. Gidi says his teachers didn't push him that hard the first year, working as they were under the assumption that he would be going home to Israel soon enough.

But Ruthie and I very clearly remember Gidi's first assignment in English class, which was to read and then write an essay about the book *To Kill a Mockingbird*. It may have been good that Gidi's teachers were not approaching his reading and writing inadequacies with any urgency, because Gidi himself quickly grew weary of the challenge all on his own.

I can remember coming home one afternoon to find Gidi lying on the couch with a cold compress over his eyes and Ruthie patiently reading to him passages from the novel. Every now and then, Gidi would let out a heavy sigh, sometimes a full groan, even an occasional "Oh my Godddd!" He'd gone from *Berenstain Bears*–level reading in English to being assigned a serious book, and he was completely overwhelmed. Ruthie thought he was going to faint.

Except for that single event, we really didn't help the kids with their homework. I like to say that my report cards are the best thing that ever happened to them. We were not hovering parents, driving them to get the best grades in school. I didn't take school seriously at their age, and because it was so easy for her, neither did Ruthie. Honestly, I was hoping they would take after Ruthie when it came to academic ability, but it was not going to bother me if they didn't.

During our second year in New York, because Gidi's school liked him so much, Chooby was invited to interview again. Ruthie refused to take him to the interview and insisted that I be the one to do it. The evening beforehand, she threatened his life—maybe not the best strategy but it worked. Knowing that the only truly valuable thing to Chooby was access to television and video games, she insisted that he control himself, or else there would be no games and no shows for a month.

This interview he passed with flying colors.

Two weeks into the new school year, I asked for a meeting with the principal of Chooby's former school—a very orthodox one. It seemed the right thing to do to explain why Chooby hadn't returned. I didn't really have a plan for what I was going to say, but I knew I wanted to end things on a good note and not have the principal take offense that we'd moved our child from an ultrareligious school to a more secular one. I ended up saying something like, "We felt strongly that we had to put Chooby in another school because he was developing a very strong attachment to Judaism and stressing out about the fact that we did not share that same attachment. Since we don't plan on becoming more religious, we decided to take him out of this school and put him in a less religious one."

"What a great success!" was the principal's cheery response.

Not only did Gidi and Chooby need to adjust to reading and writing in English; they and Ruthie needed to adjust to a much longer day at school. In Israel, school ended at one thirty in the afternoon, and there were a ton of vacation days. When we lived there, Ruthie spent an enormous amount of time with the kids at after-school activities, going to friends' houses, or hosting friends at our place. Compared with her own experience in school, she found it very disturbing that the hours the boys spent learning were so few. As a teenager, Ruthie had commuted an hour each way to the private Jewish school, where she studied thirteen subjects and three different languages, before going off to after-school activities that brought her home at around six or seven in the evening. Maybe that was too much for some kids, but *she* certainly appreciated the longer school day schedule when we moved back to New York. Education was a big deal; more school was always better than less.

In New York, just as she'd imagined, Ruthie was finally able to enjoy being a mom instead of having people everywhere tell her how horrible she was for having only two kids. To this very day, she will say to me about our sons, "So far, Chooby and Gidi have been absolutely wonderful to be around." Of course, when we moved, we missed our community in Israel. We even kept our apartment in Tel Aviv for five years so that Ruthie and the kids could summer there in the company of lots of friends. Through the years, we have kept in touch and visited back and forth with those friends, attending weddings and bar mitzvahs and sharing in one another's joys and sorrows.

Following the habit we'd set in place in Israel, we decided to make our new home as kid friendly as possible. I bought the latest video games and board games. We eventually set up a movie theater. The kids' friends were always over—eating dinner with us, hanging out, sleeping over—and we always let the boys bring friends on family vacations. We wanted to keep an eye on them as much as possible and have felt lucky that we could get to know so many of their good friends over the years. It helped, too, that Gidi's and Chooby's friends got so comfortable with us that they would sometimes sit at the dinner table and reveal everything we needed to know about what all the kids were getting up to.

Ruthie insisted that we all eat dinner together every night at seven. This she learned from her father. He owned his own business, but every single day at six o'clock, he came home for dinner with his family. She remembers the answer he gave when she asked him how it was possible: "Listen, I could stay in the office until twelve o'clock at night. There's always more to do. But I want to see my family, and I want my family to know that I'm here."

To facilitate our dinners, sometimes Leo would send Uncle Shulim on the subway to bring us meat, and Celia would often be enlisted to help cook it. Unless I was traveling, I made sure to come home and take my seat at the table.

When I did travel, Gidi would step into the "man of the house" role—presiding over dinner and then ensuring at night that all the lights were turned off and the doors locked.

CHAPTER 15

U sing Ronald's initials, we named the telecom company RSL Communications.

From my research, I knew that international calls had crazy margins that were controlled, in most countries, by monopolies. But after a while, the telecommunications industry in the US, Sweden, Finland, and some other countries experienced the lessening, and in some cases removal, of government regulations. I could see that deregulation was eventually going to occur on a global scale. That meant industries would have the leeway to operate with greater freedom, and the market would have room for more competitors.

Ronald was enthusiastic about my idea, so he got us an interview with the *New York Times* to promote our new company. I was all ready to tell the reporter our exciting story, but before the guy was even fully seated, Ronald turned to him and said, utterly straight faced, "I don't think deregulation is going to happen at all." It took me an hour just to reintroduce the legitimacy of our business idea, let alone convince the reporter that it could be successful.

Overall, I spent about six months developing the business strategy and plan. During those early months, I wanted to make some money to show Ronald that I wasn't just sitting in my office generating ideas while doing nothing to make them a reality. So, I did a small deal with Bezeq, the Israeli telecom monopoly for which I'd consulted. I purchased prepaid calling cards to sell to people traveling to Israel for use on public phones there. That project earned $20,000 in the first month. Check in hand, I marched into Ronald's CFO's office, proud of this early win. The CFO looked at the check and said, "Our accounting systems are not set up to receive money, only to spend money."

He didn't seem to be joking. Astonished, I went to Ronald.

"Makes sense" was all he said.

Ultimately, the strategy that I developed was to start operations in all the countries where deregulation had occurred as well as countries where deregulation was about to occur. Even if there were some competitors—as it turned out, there were—and even if we took only a low percentage of a huge overall market, we would still be very successful.

From my research, I had also identified that only fifteen countries accounted for 75 percent of the world's international telecom traffic. Initially, we had operations in all fifteen. Because a handful of other countries had interesting opportunities—a prepaid card operator in Denmark, for example, or an IP telephony company in Israel—we eventually expanded the number of countries to twenty-two.

Instead of building our own switches and hiring our own people, we began by purchasing 51 percent of an American reseller. That company had a great deal with a government-owned telecom company in the Dominican Republic, so carriers regularly used it to get better prices in terminating calls. Then, we started acquiring switches and starting companies around the world. At the time, Sprint was selling off companies it owned in Germany and France, so we bought those companies. In the States, a *Wall Street Journal* headline appeared: "RSL is buying Sprint," which, of course, was both far from accurate and great PR. Our third deal was with a small operation in Finland and Sweden. We put all the different operations together under one company. Combined revenues achieved a run rate of $40 million.

Then, we needed capital to expand the business, so we decided to go on a road show with Morgan Stanley to raise $100 million in debt.

That was my very first road show. I had eight meetings a day over the course of a three-week period. We visited multiple countries and states every day, meeting with the top private equity funds.

Early on, I learned an important lesson about preparing for negotiations. I would go into meetings with only a few bits of information from our bankers—the size of the fund we were about to visit, a history of types of projects funded, and the amount of money that fund tended to offer said projects. I would begin my presentation with just those few details in mind. That's all very good information, but it is nowhere near the kind of detail I would ask for as the years passed and I refined my proposal and negotiation skills. I'll say more about that later, but on this particular road show, I learned something even more basic: I learned not to underestimate my audience. Here's what happened. We went to present our company to a group of investors—all of them young twentysomethings—and I didn't take their questions seriously enough. That is to say, they asked informed and probing questions for which I did not always have answers. Instead of admitting what I didn't know and offering to get and send them the information they requested, I talked around their questions, never quite answering them directly. I offered them some bullshit in return for their attentiveness.

As soon as we left the room after that presentation, I got schooled by our banker never again to talk in circles in response to serious questions. I made amends by immediately sharing with those same investors the specific answers and information they were after. I was thankful that in the end they chose to invest.

The thing is, especially in a start-up environment, inevitably a lot of learning happens as you go. I've characterized the entire telecom enterprise during those years as a "by the seat of our pants" operation, and—perhaps because of that—I believe that every new CEO faces a big, big learning curve. The best-case scenario is that you have some good advisors, you actually learn from your experiences and develop skills over time, and you end up feeling a little more sophisticated with every new encounter and every new deal.

We ended up being offered $500 million on a $100 million raise and decided to take on $300 million in debt.

Besides having a solid business plan, I knew that I wanted to hire well, which for me has always meant surrounding myself with people much smarter than me in the functional areas for which they are responsible. I've noticed CEOs and other leaders who profess a similar management style but then really struggle to welcome and reward talent. I truly don't need to be the smartest guy in the room, but as the person in charge, I *do* need to be the guy who sets the policy for how hard decisions will be made. Then, I need to have a CFO who is the best finance person I've ever met … and heads of operations, development, R&D, sales, and so on who are better than me in each of those areas.

I was very lucky to hire an amazing management team. To support such a great team, I followed what I'd learned at Aurec and created a very specific, very family-like environment. Meaningful rewards and raises, warm and healthy daily lunches, company-wide trips, and, of course, the opportunity to participate in sports leagues. I also followed what I'd learned from consulting in Israel with the CEO of Bezeq: focus on your people, whether that means paying close attention to and rewarding the work that everyone is doing on behalf of the company or showing up with Ruthie to eight Christmas parties all in different countries across Europe and all within a ten-day period.

After one year, the company was doing well, and Ruthie and I decided to stay in New York. That summer, Ruthie took the boys to Israel to visit my parents, and I decided we needed to buy an apartment instead of continuing to rent one. The broker who had rented us our apartment had also become a friend of ours, and when I told him that I wanted to buy something, he showed me an apartment on a higher floor of our same building that was two apartments combined. Ruthie had seen the place before and liked it, so I took into consideration Ruthie's mother's advice ("If it's nice, you buy it!") and went ahead with the purchase.

The first thing I noticed was that there were so many bare walls!

When Ruthie and the boys returned, we set her up with two art consultants. She went out with them one afternoon and brought back three paintings. One was an abstract, another was of a mother and two children, and the third was a Soyer painting of a ballerina. At the time, Ruthie didn't know that Soyer was already a famous artist. That's how good an eye she's got!

That's also when I got interested in art and started doing a lot of research of my own on living artists. I've said that abstracts and landscapes don't do as much for me as artistic renderings of people. I like to be surrounded by people and to have a sense of connection to every person's story by diving a layer underneath what's available in galleries and really understanding how the artist is connected to the work.

In a sense, getting that apartment and grounding ourselves in New York opened up a whole host of opportunities for surrounding myself with more people—not only by collecting art and by building relationships but also by collecting experiences. I have that same travel bug my father had, and I can see that Chooby has it, too. Or, at the very least, he loves to go with me to the big sporting events and eat the hot dogs and the popcorn. Every game we've ever been to, we have pictures of him doing just that, with a big grin across his face. Gidi, on the other hand, has the same passion for sports as me. I've schlepped one or all our family members with me to sporting events across the world. And what started with sports (Grand Slam Championship games, Super Bowls, All-Star Games, and World Cup competitions) has expanded to include events of all kinds (Kennedy Center Honors, the Grammy Awards, the Tony Awards—I'm still trying to get us to the Oscars). It's one thing to see all those beautiful events on television; it's a completely different thing to experience them in person.

My material collections have grown accordingly—from event memorabilia (I caught a shoe that Charles Barkley signed and threw into the crowd at an All-Star Game) to little duck figurines (one from each of the sixty-nine countries in which I've so far traveled) to documents and letters written by world dignitaries and even to statues of comic superheroes. All those collections are little ways of commemorating experiences and the connections forged along the way.

Having a short commute to work helped when it came to gathering as a family for dinner each evening, especially given all the travel that was required of me in those early years. Of course, whenever I traveled, I always shopped for Ruthie and the boys. When Gidi and Chooby were young, the other kids at school would ask them where they got their clothes, and their answer was always "We get them from Dad's suitcase." Even today, I'm still proudly supplementing Ruthie's wardrobe with clothing and accessories from countries all over the world.

Starting RSL also allowed me to bring Ruthie into the business. After our first year in the US, she stopped writing for *Jane's Defence Weekly* and started working as the chief legal officer for our US subsidiary. It wasn't long before she was arranging all the contracts, building up the legal department, and reducing redundancies and inefficiencies. I'd be running around making deals, and she'd be running right behind me, papering them as quickly as she could. She liked working as general counsel, sitting in on all the business meetings, giving her opinions about the legal aspects of our projects. Then, when RSL USA had to move from Long Island into the city, she got to put her real estate purchasing skills to work locating a sublet on Forty-Sixth and Park that was dirt cheap. Soon thereafter, when a local magazine tried to call RSL USA to account for seeming to overspend on office space and not investing in its people and services—"How dare you locate your US offices on Park Avenue! And how dare your parent company sit beside Ronald Lauder in the GM Building, the 'Taj Mahal' of New York!"—she laughed at the unfoundedness of the criticism.

CHAPTER 16

In those days, everyone in telecom was looking to make a quick buck. And all these characters jumped into the market. Some became wealthy. A lot lost their shirts. Some turned into crooks.

At first, we were competing against the incumbents, the AT&Ts and Bells of the world. Then, as the market opened up and more and more companies came on the scene, Voice over Internet Protocol, or VoIP, a technology that allowed people to make voice calls over the internet rather than over a phone line, became a reliable tool and introduced a whole new generation of competitors.

A lot has changed between then and today, but it's still the case now that legacy clients (clients of companies that still have switches and landlines) are radically overpaying for services. Today, if you dial internationally without a plan, you are likely to be charged over a dollar a minute. But the cost for the carrier is less than one cent. Most people don't know that it's very possible to get a VoIP subscription with unlimited international calling for as little as twelve dollars a month.

Not knowing is what allows money to be made. When people don't understand—or misunderstand—how the market works, there will always be a big business opportunity.

At RSL, we were very smart to be in the right places at the right time, with markets opening up and the ability to raise a lot of money for the company. A year after we raised debt and put it to work for us, we had over $100 million in revenue, and three years after that, $1.2 billion. In October 1997, we went public with a billion-dollar valuation, and within an overall period of seven years, we made thirty-seven acquisitions, from carrier-to-carrier companies, to prepaid calling cards, to operators that serve small- and medium-sized businesses as well as the VoIP companies.

Let me take a step back to give you a better sense of that growth process. You'll recall that one of our initial moves was to ensure that we owned switches in the fifteen countries responsible for most of the world's calling traffic. Now, if we had done only that—if we had *only* grown organically by accumulating clients and innovating our product line—expanding the company would have been a very painful process, especially after we went public and were held to a stricter set of revenue targets. It would have taken us twenty-five years to do what we did in a quarter of that time.

We grew as quickly as we did through targeted acquisitions, buying companies with products that we could absorb or that offered us an opportunity for sense-making expansion outside the primary countries in which we did business. I should say that buying companies and successfully integrating them is no small task. But instead of relying only on chasing cutting-edge advances in the field, acquisition relies more on possessing solid capacities, plans, and practices for integration. It wouldn't be good, for example, to acquire five—or thirty-five—different companies with all different platforms, billing systems, and other processes. It's almost never okay to acquire aggressively without also creating a cohesive operation among all one's assets. And just as there has to be a reliable strategy for merging companies, partnerships should also be truly strategic—offering clear collaborative benefits, real complementarity, enhanced capabilities, and revenue share—for both parties.

The business of taking the company public required a second road show, though raising equity is, of course, different from raising debt. When people own debt, they simply want to be repaid; when people own equity, they want the company's value to increase.

There were some challenges on that journey, both anticipated and unanticipated.

We had an excellent management team, but they had no experience taking a company public. To get around what would certainly be an issue for our investors, Ronald's ex-CFO, a former partner at Goldman Sachs, agreed to be the CFO for the public offering. Our existing CFO, Mark Hirschhorn, did all the work, mind you, but having brought on a guy who looked fantastic on paper did us a world of good.

The next obstacle was that Ronald insisted we go public on a billion-dollar valuation. Typically, it's best to take a company public at a price that everybody thinks is a bargain for them. You generate the buzz that the shares are undervalued, and then, when your valuation goes up from there, everyone is happy and you sell more shares. But because our initial valuation was so high, our shares never flew. In the years that followed, there was little demand for the stock, and we mostly hovered around that same high price at which we'd started. Not a bad situation, but not the best.

Also not a bad situation, but not the best, was Ronald's interest in being an active participant in key money-raising events for the company. I appreciated but hadn't anticipated that Ronald saw RSL as his big play as a businessman. His mother had great success in the world of cosmetics, and he decided he was going to have great success in the world of telecommunications.

Now, on the way to going public, there are two major investor conferences, one held in Boston, second only to the one held in New York City. Ronald decided to speak at the Boston luncheon, anticipating that he would then also speak at the big event in New York.

At the luncheon in Boston, he approached the podium and began, "My mother started a cosmetics company. I started a telecom company."

Then, he paused for what felt like a whole minute, fussing with the pages of his remarks all the while.

My CFO, Mark, who was sitting beside me, took that moment to write a note on the pages in his lap: "The meltdown in Chernobyl is nothing compared to what we are witnessing here."

Ronald's next words were "Somebody mixed up my pages."

Eventually he got the pages in order and completed his remarks.

Luckily, and because he's Ronald Lauder—a man of great generosity and exquisite taste—the investors were very enthusiastic to see him, and it didn't hurt us at all. We got great offers.

But as we were leaving, our banker from Goldman Sachs took Ronald aside to say, "Ronald, if you want the company to have a successful IPO, you're not speaking in New York."

Ronald nodded in acknowledgment.

Looking back on it now, I can say that we didn't have any trouble raising money before taking RSL Communications public. Please don't misunderstand me—it was as exhausting as any fundraising effort is likely to be. We traveled extensively across the globe, and once again I had to give some version of the same presentation eight times a day. Occasionally, there were unexpected differences in otherwise routine encounters with prospective investors. In Switzerland, somebody asked me if my accent was from Texas, and I was able to incorporate that detail for laughs in the many presentations that followed. During another presentation, the fellow with whom we were meeting fell asleep for a whole handful of minutes.

At other times, conversations would veer off track, clearly going nowhere, as when in a meeting with high-level investors in South Korea, the investors persisted in inquiring about the silliest of things.

About Ronald, they asked the following:

"Does he have a movie theater in his house?"

"Yes."

"Does he have many houses?"

"Yes."

And of me, they asked, "Where are you from?"

"Germany." It was so clear to me that there would be no deal that I couldn't help but lie.

"Is it true that in the north of Germany they talk with a lot of *xxcccch* sounds and in the south of Germany they talk more like …"

I decided to lean into the ridiculousness.

"No, no, no. You've got it all wrong! In the south of Germany they talk with a lot of *xxcccch* sounds, and in the north …"

They were not the right partners for us, but I think we did good work keeping our sense of humor.

Differences in our road show presentations might reflect distinct cultural differences. Before traveling to Japan, for example, I learned about the importance of not showing the soles of my shoes in a business meeting and not offering anyone a watch as a gift, as these gestures have offensive and threatening interpretations in that culture. But what I didn't know was that their response to our full pitch would involve pretending they didn't hear a word we said and then asking a series of questions that essentially forced us to run through the entirety of the pitch again.

A final unanticipated difference involved situations where it seemed we weren't going to secure an investment and someone would ask me to answer broad speculative questions like "What do you think the company's earnings will be in five years?" In each instance, I would generate some nonsense answer or other. Thankfully, our head of business development started writing down what we said in each country so that, on the off chance that one of these seeming "no-go" pitches eventually garnered some interest, we would be able to respond consistently to each.

When it came, however, to *intentional* differences in road show presentations, I made sure to learn from past experience. I didn't, for example, make assumptions about the credibility or authority of our audiences, and I was sure to respond honestly if there happened to be a question I could not answer.

And this time around, I added a third lesson to the others: I learned that every CEO trying to sell shares talks about how great their management team is. Knowing that I needed to make us stand out from all the other companies that would be proposing themselves to essentially the same set of investors, I shared specific claims about members of our management team. Instead of saying something trite like "We have a fabulous management team!" I featured individual team members and said things about them that truly distinguished their careers or efforts and successes at RSL Communications. I wanted everyone with whom we met to understand that I had hired world-class talent, even if I knew that talent had yet to add to their résumés the experience of taking a company public.

A highlight of the whole effort was one you might not expect: I relied on my mother to help us raise money. We had recently invested in a company called Delta 3 that conducted voice calls over the internet, and I would contact my mother in every meeting to show off the quality of the calls. Why did I do that? Because I knew she would be at home to answer every single call. One of the bankers asked, "How is it possible she's always there?" No matter how little time had passed between one call and the next, she always had something new to say. I may not have been surprised that she was always at home to pick up the call, but even *I* was astounded that she could generate a fresh conversation each time. I'd think to myself, *I just talked with you an hour ago!* as she conveyed an update about my grandfather's health or told me about some new dish she was preparing.

At the end of every day of the road show, the bankers told us how many orders they had in their books so that we would know exactly how we were doing. We found out later that they never gave us the right numbers—in this case because they didn't want us to be full of ourselves. But before the last day of presentations, they told us the truth: we were oversubscribed, which was a very good problem to have.

Our last day of meetings was hilarious to me, because our bankers hated what I did. I started all my presentations with the caveat "The bankers told me yesterday that we are oversubscribed. So, I'm here today because it was scheduled for us to meet. But I'm not sure we're going to be able to allocate any shares for you."

On that final day, we got more orders than on any other.

In a funny sense, road shows are a bit like dating. If you tell the person you're courting that you are crazy about them, it's likely they will not be interested. If you tell them that you don't need them, they are crazy about you. Even in business, playing hard to get is a good tactic.

Compared to today, raising money was remarkably easy back then. I remember one raise, which took place when the company was already publicly traded, when our CFO called me the night before to say, "You can raise four hundred million tomorrow if you agree to do a one-hour call at lunchtime." That sort of thing doesn't happen with any frequency in the market today.

We may never have struggled to raise money, but given that the management team and I were rookies at taking a company public, we still had some lessons to learn about our access to it.

We all learned quickly that careful scrutiny is made of the actions taken by the management team in relation to its shares in the company. If management starts selling shares, it's a bad sign for the market. Immediately, the public will think you don't believe in your own company, and people will follow suit by dumping their shares, too. So, the general rule was something like "Don't sell shares."

This was not a popular rule, because not getting rid of shares meant we couldn't really benefit from our stock in the company. That's when I learned about a vehicle called an exchange fund. Essentially, you put your restricted shares into a shared fund; you're not selling them per se but rather exchanging large holdings of a single stock to participate in the fund's entire portfolio of investments. Now, you cannot sell your shares in this fund for five years, but your shares are in a basket holding 120 companies' shares. So, even though I could not sell any of my holdings in the fund for five years, I was protecting the value of the shares I contributed.

At the time, however, nobody really understood how those funds worked, and I was counseled against participating in one and considered an outlier when I chose to do so anyway. Later, other systems were developed, like the one that offers management the opportunity to sell off a certain number of shares every quarter during an open window for trading. The idea there is that you sell shares automatically for the current price when that window opens. Today, all CEOs and other insiders put themselves on this kind of plan, and nobody questions it.

I put a chunk of my RSL shares into an exchange fund and got lucky. When I look at what I put into the fund then and what it has appreciated to today, I can say that if I ever found myself in another situation where I had restricted shares, I would put those into an exchange fund as well. To me, it's been a savvy way to increase our family's financial security.

Not long after going public, two rather interesting things happened with our investment in Delta 3, the VoIP company I mentioned earlier. The first involves Gustavo Cisneros, a famous Venezuelan businessman who had invested $50 million in RSL. We held one of our board meetings in Caracas, and Cisneros was a lovely host, treating the group to very fancy meals. At the board meeting itself, I presented Delta 3 for the first time, pointing out that we had paid $5 million for 51 percent of the company.

"We are talking about a cutting-edge technology," I said.

Heads nodded with enthusiasm, and that's when Cisneros stood up and said, "You are talking about new technologies. I would like to introduce all of you to a new technology that was developed in Venezuela." He opened his arms wide in a grand gesture toward the doors of our conference room. They flung open, and in came the twelve finalists in the Miss Venezuela pageant. Cisneros owned the competition and the number one television channel on which it aired. The "technology," we soon learned, was that all the contestants were scouted from villages across the country and then put into a preparatory school for a year, during which time they learned the skills necessary for competing in the pageant in addition to undergoing whatever surgeries were deemed necessary to make them appear flawless. The room full of male board members had no trouble showing great appreciation for Cisneros's new technology.

The second interesting detail is that when it became clear that RSL would go forward on a billion-dollar valuation, Delta 3's founders came to my office insisting on selling us the other 49 percent of their company and receiving RSL shares.

"You are making a mistake," I said, "because I am eventually going to take Delta 3 public on its own."

"You are lying to us," they yelled and made it clear they would only settle for selling the other half of the company to RSL.

So, I bought them for another $5 million.

A year or so afterward, I nominated Mark Hirschhorn as CFO, and he took Delta 3 public at a valuation of $350 million. A few months after that, the company reached a billion-dollar valuation. The founders would have made around $490 million if they'd heeded my advice.

Instead, they were devastated. I had been trying to help them, but they missed a big opportunity by insisting on rolling their shares.

"You never know in life," I always say. I'm a big believer that luck plays a sizeable role in business success, but you have to be able to create opportunities and, as in this instance, run with the ones that present themselves.

CHAPTER 17

RSL was an amazing adventure. It was my first experience starting a company from scratch, serving as CEO, and eventually growing the company to over four thousand employees in twenty-two countries with over $1 billion in revenues. On top of that, I got to see Ruthie find legal work that she actually enjoyed. I made lifelong friends while at RSL, and I am and will be forever grateful to Ronald Lauder for investing in my idea and giving me the opportunity of a lifetime.

Maybe it's for those reasons that I can't leave off talking about that period in our lives until I've given a fuller picture of the extent of Ronald's influence over the course of those seven years.

Ronald's commitment to Judaism reaches far and wide; even back when I started working with him in the mid-1990s, he had already spent a fortune to preserve Jewish heritage and revitalize Jewish life across Eastern Europe. One of the things he did (which drove the Polish government crazy) was to purchase a street in Warsaw that had been part of the Jewish ghetto. Ronald refused to change anything about the street; he wanted people to be able to come and experience what remained of it. In the end, the Polish government couldn't take it any longer; the street has a shopping mall on it now.

When Ronald invited me to join him in Poland at the 1995 International March of the Living, I jumped at the opportunity. The march, which happens every year, involves a series of educational programs as well as an organized walk down the path from Auschwitz to Birkenau in tribute to all victims of the Holocaust.

At Auschwitz, we witnessed the barracks where Leo and Celia had slept. When I phoned them from there, Celia answered the phone but wouldn't respond to me. "I'm here," I said into the receiver. "I'm here." But she was completely silent.

I wasn't supposed to, but I collected a rock from each crematorium that we visited. At one point, I also casually dug into the ground and unearthed a warped metal spoon. In our apartment, these items are preserved under glass, and they sit atop a big book that has the word *Jew* written in it six million times. We keep them in the kitchen, where we can see them throughout the day, in the very place we take sustenance.

By 1998, I had convinced Leo to go along with me to the march. He had refused to return to Poland, but when I told him that Ronald Lauder had invited him to travel on his private jet, Leo finally acquiesced. We took Gidi with us, too, who was a junior in high school at the time. The little group of us went to the march, and Leo visited the barracks in which he'd been held. Witnessing Leo's response to being there was a surreal experience for all of us. There were, of course, other survivors all around us, and many of them were comparing the numbers tattooed on their arms. Leo found a man whose number was just ten behind his own.

Then we traveled to Kielce to see the house Leo had lived in and the school he and Shulim attended. Leo was a small man, but I noticed that he was walking tall during most of the experience. It may have helped that I had invited Doron, who has the stature of a bodyguard, to come along on the trip. In point of fact, I'd asked

Doron to come along because he was a medic, and I was worried about Leo's physical well-being coming face to face with his past. With Doron walking alongside us, both Leo and I felt more at ease, albeit for very different reasons.

That said, when a drunk Pole started screaming at us along the road, Leo looked like he had been transported backward in time, freshly experiencing the deep hatred against us. Thankfully, Doron walked ahead of us and shooed the screaming man out of the way.

I decided it was important to take Chooby next, so when he was a high school junior, I arranged for his whole class to go to the March of the Living. We brought Ruthie's uncle Josie with us, too.

Josie, the intellectual, was an absolute font of memories. We were walking in Warsaw, and he was able to point to every building and identify who had lived there—this family in this house, that family in that one. The businesses that had been here and there. Every street, every building, he knew.

Josie broke down numerous times. But then, while we were standing near the memorial of the Warsaw ghetto uprising and watching a ceremony with several hundred Israeli soldiers, a Pole walking his dog along the perimeter flipped his cigarette butt into the center of the square.

Josie walked right up to the man and in Polish said to him, "You know, this is a holy place. Please pick up your cigarette."

When Josie returned, I said to him jokingly, "If you didn't have two hundred Israeli soldiers around you, would you have asked that man to pick up his cigarette?"

On my fourth visit to Poland, I dragged Ruthie there for the first and only time. Celia had made Ruthie swear that she would never visit the country, but Ruthie had grown up listening to all the stories, and I thought she would find it valuable to see what she'd already heard so much about. We brought our good friends Eti and Yair with us so that Ruthie would have additional moral support.

The important thing to know about Ruthie is that you cannot detach her from her handbag. It's large, it weighs a ton, and it's got everything in it—it's her Mary Poppins accessory. When the kids were growing up, absolutely anything they asked for could be found in that bag.

"Do you have a Band-Aid?"

"Of course!"

"Do you have a cookie?"

"Sure, which kind would you like? I have this one, these … oh, and this."

"Do you have a sandwich?"

And on it would go. Today, as I draft these pages, she's on her way to visit our grandchildren, carrying lamb chops, gnocchi, vegetables, and who knows what else.

I was well aware of Ruthie's commitment to her handbag, but I'd forgotten to take it into consideration until we arrived at the gates to Auschwitz. At the entrance, the guards require visitors to leave their bags in nearby lockers.

Up to this point in our visit, Ruthie had been extremely calm, but when they told her she had to store the handbag, she had a fit. "My parents were at this camp. I lost all my relatives at this camp. And you are not touching my handbag!"

They were scared enough that they let her keep it. I think hers might have been the only handbag ever allowed into Auschwitz.

At the same time that Ronald helped deepen our family's understanding of the history of Judaism in Europe, he also provided me the opportunity to develop a fuller sense of my immediate connections to the political scene in Israel. I have to say, the latter was far more confusing to me overall.

When we started RSL, Ronald was then very good friends with Bibi Netanyahu; the two had grown close during the period when Bibi was an ambassador to the United Nations. So, when Bibi was nominated as prime minister for the first time, Ronald and I flew to Israel to congratulate him. On our arrival, however, I was informed that I was not allowed into the meeting room.

Ronald went in on his own, and when he came out, he looked to me a bit funereal. I learned that Bibi was utterly uninterested in any advice Ronald had to give about the responsibilities of his new post; instead, Bibi insulted Ronald by encouraging him to keep sending expensive clothes and gifts. Bibi's wife, Sarah, was also part of the conversation, and Ronald recalled her saying that she and Bibi were going to be the Charles and Diana of Israel. I was not let in to congratulate Bibi, because Sarah was upset with me. To this day, I have no idea why.

About six months later, Ronald called me into his office to say that he did not want my relationship with Bibi to be ruined because of Sarah. "I have figured out with their lawyer how we are going to fix it!" he announced.

"How are we going to fix it?" I have to say, I was curious.

"We are going to buy Sarah a present."

"I'm not buying her a present."

"No, of course not. *I'm* buying her a present, but it will be as if *you* bought her a present, and then *we'll* send it to her."

"You can do whatever you want. I'm not doing it."

Ronald bought Sarah a Tiffany clock and sent it with a note that read, "To Sarah, the mother of the nation of Israel."

Shortly after it arrived, I received a call from Ronald with the following instruction: "Go to Israel. Bibi wants to see you."

I went, and it was as if nothing at all had happened.

Six months later, an investigation began into gifts that Bibi and Sarah received. I got a call from Bibi, who said into the receiver, "I'm in Moscow on my way to see Putin. Do you remember the present you sent?"

"What present?" I asked, genuinely not remembering.

"Exactly."

And that was the entirety of the call.

I would learn much more about Ronald's investment interests after departing from RSL, but while I was still CEO of the company, he received a call from then-mayor of Jerusalem Ehud Olmert, who later became prime minister, asking Ronald to buy the city's soccer team. That team was known throughout Israel to have the most fanatic fans ever.

Olmert pitched Ronald, "This team has the widest fan base in the whole country. Owning it would put you on the map in Israel, give you excellent PR. Everybody will know and love you."

Ronald proposed to me that the two of us do this deal fifty-fifty and asked me to check it out in greater detail. Ruthie and I happened to be in Israel at the time, so we went to a game. Olmert was right that the fans were fanatics; they were singing and shouting the whole time. I was invited to speak to the players at halftime, and Ruthie and I got to sit beside the chairman of the soccer association. This was distressing for Ruthie, because the man ate sunflower seeds obsessively and was spitting the shells all over the place.

Afterward, I called Olmert and asked, "How much debt does the team have?"

"Five million." The city had been giving the team money to help it get by, but that wasn't enough to sustain it.

I hired an accounting firm. After two weeks of due diligence, the accountants found $20 million in debt and still hadn't finished their search.

Of course, Ronald and I were no longer interested in the deal.

Olmert was not at all pleased and threatened to ruin our reputations. According to him, we would never again be able to step into the city of Jerusalem. The fans would never forgive us. Our photos had been in the newspaper when we were entertaining the offer to buy the team, and then we were in the newspaper just as much, if not more, for having turned down the opportunity. Around that time, I was in Israel for another visit, so I went to another game—and brought my strong and tall friend Doron with me—to see if the fallout was in fact as Olmert had promised. While we were there, I received a call from Ronald.

He called at precisely the moment when a stadium full of twenty-five thousand people were chanting and singing, "Ronald Lauder's mother is a whore."

"Listen," I said, holding the phone up to the crowd. "Can you hear that?"

"What are they singing?"

"Ronald, they are blessing your mother."

Late in my career as CEO of RSL, I had a surreal experience while entertaining deals with Ronald. Little did I know it would set the tone for the two years that followed my departure from the company.

Ronald received a call that Slobodan Milošević—who had become president of Yugoslavia in 1997 and who was, of course, a killer—wanted us to visit Belgrade to discuss a deal that would give RSL all the international telecom traffic for Yugoslavia. Our lawyers informed us that there was a US boycott on doing business with the

Yugoslavian government, but since RSL was a Bermuda-registered company, we were cleared to visit and listen to the offer.

Ronald would travel from the US to Belgrade, and I was traveling from Israel on a private jet sent by Milošević; we were to meet in a hotel not far from the government buildings. Our conversation with Milošević was supposed to be hush-hush, thoroughly secret, but before I deplaned in Belgrade, someone from Milošević's staff came on board and presented himself to me as the head of ceremony, or some such thing. From there, I was guided to a car, and an entire motorcade took me to the hotel. I entered the hotel lobby to see two giant banners featuring huge photos of me and Ronald.

I comprehended that we were already in deep shit, but I was also exhausted and eager to sleep. Ronald had yet to arrive from the US, so we were going to have to discuss everything the next day.

The following morning, I turned on the TV in my room, and all over the news I saw our photos and heard announcements and speculations about our visit: Fisher/Lauder, Lauder/Fisher—on every channel! In that moment, I came to understand something I had not realized beforehand: nobody from the US had visited former Yugoslavia in some time; our presence was nothing short of a very big deal.

The rest of the visit was a blur of strange exchanges. First, we were taken to meet the minister for telecommunications. We listened politely, and when the doors to our meeting room opened, a slew of reporters came rushing in, eager to ask us for details. We were able to avoid their curiosity only because we were already being ushered into a conference of the foreign ministers of the Balkan countries. That's when I learned that I would be speaking to all of them about the telecom industry.

What the hell am I doing here? I wondered, but my training as a spokesman for the Israel Defense Forces kicked in, and I accomplished my task with no trouble.

From there, our host, who was the head of the secret service, took Ronald and me to meet Milošević himself. We were ushered into a big office with tall windows and a separate sitting area. Milošević started the conversation by telling us that he was happy to give RSL all the country's international traffic. His proposal was that in exchange for becoming friends forever in this way, we would grant him a little favor. Apparently assuming that we either did or could control the US Congress, the favor he asked was nothing less than for us to call off US boycotts and sanctions against his country.

That's when Ronald, feeling emboldened to use his diplomatic negotiation skills, said something like this to Milošević: "You know, you should give back Kosovo. Look at the Jews in Israel. They gave back Hebron to the Palestinian Authority, and you can give back Kosovo to Serbia. Really, it's not such a big deal."

No sooner had Ronald finished his sentence than our host leaned over to him and said, "For us, Kosovo is not Hebron. It is Jerusalem."

"Oh, Jerusalem?" Ronald paused for a moment and then added, "Don't give up Kosovo!"

By then, I'd started to feel like I was sitting inside an alien spaceship. I excused myself to the restroom and returned just in time for the meeting to finish and for Milošević to walk us to our car and motorcade.

As we were settling into our seats, the head of the secret service said to us, "Listen, I have two things to tell you. First, we measure meetings with Milošević like this: If he does not get up from the chair, the meeting is a disaster. If he gets up from the chair and walks you to the door, it is a very good meeting. If he walks you a little bit outside the door—amazing meeting. In my whole history with him, he has never walked anyone to the car. Second, in my whole career, I have never seen anyone leave a meeting with him to take a bathroom break."

Not that long after Ronald and I returned to New York, an article appeared in the *New York Times* claiming that we had signed a commercial deal in defiance of US policy. The state department even started an investigation into us, but obviously we hadn't done any deals. We had just shown up to listen to the proposal—deeply strange as the circumstances of that visit had been.

CHAPTER 18

T elecom had its moment. A lot of people made money. And then, a lot of businesses hit the wall. Governments across the globe decided that telecom expenses were ridiculous and the margins too high, so they incentivized the lowering of prices. It became harder to raise money when all the big carriers decided to get rid of their small- and medium-sized competitors by lowering prices. Even some of the largest telecom companies disappeared entirely.

About eight months before I left the company, we went out to raise money again. It was a tougher road show because the markets had started to be in trouble, but we followed the plan the bankers had set and we made it by the skin of our teeth. We hit the amount we were trying to raise—and not a penny more.

The bankers told us it had helped that I tried to get to know the people I was talking to and endeavored to leave them with a unique and memorable impression. And it's true—my attitude had changed some. I'd started to think about the road shows and other business negotiation processes as a bit like art collecting. Just as with collecting, my inclination was to learn the story behind the image, so in business, too, I started taking more time with people, getting to know them better, looking for opportunities to genuinely bond and establish solid trust. What might we discover we had in common, and how might I see them differently once I learned their stories?

The trouble with raising that last bit of money was that it was clear the company would need even more in order to survive. What we had set ourselves up to raise wasn't going to be enough, and no more money was available. I struggled to sleep at night. I regularly felt sick to my stomach. I can say, today, that no period in my professional life was more stressful. As Ruthie tells it, I was very upset right up until the end. I'd built a thriving company with more than four thousand employees—then the market changed, and difficult decisions had to be made. I knew that in order to save the company, a lot of people would be let go. I also knew I was not the right guy to undertake that process. I decided that I had been the company's *growth guy* and that I needed to recruit a *restructuring guy* to take my place. I didn't have the heart for downsizing and integrating in this instance.

So, I convinced the company's board that we needed to bring in a restructuring person to head the company—someone unburdened by a sense of personal obligation to employees, someone who could just focus on the numbers and do what was necessary. The board appointed me head of the search committee to find my successor. That was a tough process, too, but the guy I hired did what needed to be done; he came in without any commitments to any of the employees and focused on the bottom line and the board's approved plan. He did his best until the board eventually decided to break up the business and sell its assets.

When I left RSL, I asked to have the compensation I was owed spread out over two years, and then I asked Ronald for a small space in his office suite. My intention was to spend those two years getting my sea legs as a private investor and consulting with Ronald, offering whatever business assistance he needed from me.

I started investing close to home, so to speak, by dabbling in telecom. I put together a group of investors and bought a company called PSINet that had $700 million invested in it but was losing $1 million a month. We bought the company in bankruptcy court for $9.5 million, and when we started looking at all its accounts, we found that the company had $24 million and owned a couple of buildings. We sold the buildings and used the cash to make the company profitable: we cut out services in the countries where the company was losing money, we better integrated its acquisitions, and we devised more efficient operating systems. Here was one way I *could* be a restructuring guy. A year and a half later, we sold the company to a government-owned Australian telecom company for $120 million.

Then, when RSL started selling its assets, a couple of partners and I purchased its Finnish operation. That was a profitable company with about $15 million a year in revenues. We bought it for $7.5 million, cleaned up its functionality the same way we had with PSINet, and then sold it for over $60 million eighteen months later.

I learned that when something has fallen totally out of favor and nobody wants to touch it, there are always crazy opportunities. Besides that, we were coming into these businesses knowing exactly what we were doing. Buying into something and flipping it, getting in and out in a handful of years, and moving on to the next project was fun work and fitting to my personality.

I did a bit of consulting for Goldman Sachs during those years, and Ruthie and I got involved in a few real estate investment projects as well: buying and renovating property and finding a suitable apartment for Gidi when he finished college.

During that same time frame, the people close to Ronald—his chief of staff, his brother, his oldest daughter, his son-in-law—assigned me a very specific task in relation to his business activities: kill all the new deals that Ronald was considering. Given that I'd offered to advise Ronald, mine would be the expert opinion that could help influence his decision-making. His family believed he should focus on his work in the arts; this was the area in which he had both deep knowledge and great talent as well as a true ability for making money. It was also very much not an area in which he sought my advice.

Let me remind you that I believed one of my strengths was spotting good deals and then achieving good results with them. But when it came to Ronald, I had been put in charge of squelching his interest rather than cultivating it. For the two years that I worked very closely with him, I came to understand that he was so generous and so broadly interested in the business world that he got thoroughly excited about nearly any idea nearly anyone proposed to him. And, wow, did ideas of all kinds come across his desk. I could be sitting in my office any afternoon and be called to join him in a series of unscheduled meetings with people proposing business deals left and right.

What does it take to kill a deal? Anything from zero effort to something more considerable.

Ronald had hired a man named Chris Bogart specifically *to make* deals and protect his investments, so Chris became my partner in crime, at least to the extent that he and I would both recognize when an opportunity was not a good one. Early on, Ronald sent the two of us to Bulgaria to determine whether he should buy nuclear plants there. Bulgaria was joining the EU at the time. Up to that point, its electricity had been provided by Russian nuclear plants, but one of the conditions for Bulgaria joining the union was to shut down those plants. Ronald's creative solution—one I'm sure no one else would even have considered—was to buy the plants, and then the government of Bulgaria would buy electricity from him instead of from the Russians.

So, Chris and I went to negotiate the deal; we met with the king and the minister of finance, and everyone seemed in favor of proceeding. But the key meeting would take place with the management team of the three nuclear plants themselves. That team had decided to hold the meeting in a ski resort. It was summertime, and nobody would be there.

As we were being driven to the resort, I looked over to see Chris typing away on his Blackberry, texting his wife: "I'm going to message you every half hour. If you don't hear from me on schedule, alert the police. It means I am either kidnapped or dead."

Despite Chris's anxiety, we arrived intact, witnessed the managers' presentation about revenues, profits, and so on, and then listened to their closing remarks. They ended by asserting that if Ronald purchased the nuclear plants, he would never see any profit from them.

Chris started to analyze the numbers and asked, "Why is that? There is so much profit here and here, and there …"

Their answer: "All this profit we are keeping for ourselves. We don't care if you're buying or not buying. There will be no profit for you."

In that moment, I understood that the deal was dead; there was nothing I would have to do to kill it. But to my surprise, Chris continued to negotiate through the rest of the night. It wasn't until morning that he was convinced no deal was there.

The next big trip Chris and I took was to Kyiv, because Ronald was very excited about owning a bank in Ukraine and had found a Jewish family willing to sell to him. Again, there was no deal—but this time for different reasons. There were at least 250 different banks—the government gave out licenses left and right—and joining a market with hundreds of other similar competitors is never a good business idea. We had a lovely dinner with the family and then returned home the next day to tell Ronald there would be no deal.

After that, an opportunity arose in Romania. This time, Ronald invited me and Fred Langhammer, who was the CEO of Estée Lauder at the time, to join in his investment. Ronald told us he had already signed an exclusive deal to distribute gasoline to about a million and a half citizens, all living within a specific area of the country.

Of course, Fred and I started asking questions like "Do they have good infrastructure to get the gas to the houses?" We didn't learn much from Ronald's responses, so we transitioned to "What is the deal they're offering?"

"I paid five million up front, and I have to pay another ten million upon completion of due diligence."

"Why did you pay five million when you haven't even checked out the opportunity yet?"

"No, no, no. There were many parties interested. I had to get it."

On this occasion, Fred traveled solo. He was already headed to Europe and promised to stop by Romania and do the due diligence.

When Fred returned, it took me a while to understand what he was saying because he was laughing so hard between words and sentences. The company in which Ronald had invested amounted to a couple of trucks delivering gas canisters to a handful of houses. It was true that the company had the rights to service the whole area, but there was absolutely no infrastructure to support their plan.

When Fred settled down, he advised Ronald, "Write off the five million that you've given them, and don't even come close to this deal."

With deals like these and help from Chris and Fred, killing business opportunities seemed easy enough.

After a while, Ronald asked me to look into chemical trading, so I brought him a chemical trader. That also was easy enough to do, as I had myself just invested in a chemical trading company called Kemlink. I invited the CEO of that company to talk with Ronald.

In our meeting, the guy offered Ronald a warning: "In chemical trading, it is easy to turn a very big fortune into a very small fortune."

"In this, I am an expert," said Ronald, smiling wryly.

When I invested in Kemlink, I was introduced to a man in Finland who also dealt in chemicals. So, for my own sake, I reached out to schedule a meeting with him. He invited me to Monte Carlo, where he would also be meeting up with the partners in his investment circle, a group trading oil out of Russia.

So, Chris, Ruthie, and I schlepped ourselves to Monte Carlo. I knew before we went that the guy we were there to meet had once been head of the KGB in Finland, but what I did not know is that the others in his group were also high-ranking ex-KGB officials.

Ruthie and I met with my contact and his Finnish mistress for coffee. I noticed that he was wearing a $100,000 Constantin watch and complimented it. This was our first meeting ever, but he nonchalantly removed the watch from his wrist, handed it to me, and said, "Here, a present for you." Having some experience with business deals, I well knew such a present would inevitably have strings attached. I refused as politely as I could, and we continued to talk. Before we parted, he invited us to a dinner for the group of investors at Le Louis XV—Alain Ducasse.

At dinner, we were seated at a long table, about twenty of us in total. Next to Ruthie sat a man named Konstantin, who we learned was based in Moscow and managed a telecom company with $60 million in revenue and $40 million in profit. Since the company was supplying the Russian government and its army, those numbers explained Konstantin's real role: the petty cash person in Putin's circle. From those revenues and profits, he provided the dinners, the watches, the mistresses' jewelry and apartments—whatever the group needed.

Konstantin took great care to tell us about everyone at the table and their respective high-level roles in the KGB. Ruthie and I both liked Konstantin a lot, but I could see the slight transitions in Ruthie's and Chris's demeanors as different members of the group were named and their roles acknowledged. Until then, I don't think it had quite occurred to Ruthie the company we were keeping.

Ruthie started kicking me under the table and murmuring, "Killers," under her breath.

But Chris? I knew he was saying goodbye to his life again, but this time instead of furiously texting his wife, he simply presented a cheery, interested smile and started knocking back glasses of expensive champagne.

The dinner was long, easily lasting five hours. Each time we believed it was coming to an end, someone would order more champagne, more caviar, more this or that. In the end, the bill was extraordinary. As we walked back to our hotel, I learned that Ruthie had been concerned we might all be gunned down through the very large windows framing our table. Chris, by then drunk on champagne, laughed out loud and admitted that he had imagined something similar.

The next day, we were invited to a meeting at the Finnish mistress's apartment. I went ahead of Ruthie to spend time discussing how we might all work together. When she gave her taxi driver the address of the apartment, he turned to her and said, "It's not possible. Nobody lives there." The apartment, it turned out, was right next door to Prince Albert's palace.

"Well, take me there anyway," Ruthie suggested. When they arrived at the address, the driver insisted on waiting for her, still convinced there was no way she could be in the right place. She rang the bell a few times before someone came, opened it, and welcomed her in. And when she turned to thank the driver, she saw that he was in shock that an American tourist knew of a location in the area that he did not. "I can't believe it!" she heard him say as she passed through the entranceway.

No concrete plans were made on that trip, but later Chris and I were invited for another social visit with my contact in Finland. I felt proud that for all his hesitations, Chris continued to accompany me on trips like these.

The minute we arrived at our host's dacha on the lake, there was champagne. The three of us talked a bit, and then there was vodka, then an aperitif, and then some cognac. Then it was time to go shooting. Chris gave me a look that let me know he was panicking again. But our host put out some targets, we shot at them, and we returned to the dacha for more drinking.

Our host smoked some fish for our dinner. As mealtime approached, we were required to transition to drinking whiskey. The entire annual Finnish quota for twenty-five-year-old Macallan whiskey went to our contact, which meant he had an entire basement full of it. I could feel I was not myself from all the drinking; Chris, on the other hand, had committed to drinking champagne the entire time, so although he was anxious, he was also not drunk.

Before the meal commenced, our host announced, "Now, we have to do a sauna!" So, of course, we put on woolen caps and sat in the sauna for ten minutes before being directed, "And now, we jump into the lake!" Together, we ran out of the sauna and onto the ice. Our host quickly smashed a pick into the ice, and we jumped into the bit of water that his hacking had exposed. Then it was back to the sauna for another ten minutes. We repeated this routine three times. After three times, I was not drunk anymore. In fact, I felt sharper than ever before in my entire life. And that smoked fish was some of the best I've ever tasted.

The deal that was proposed to me—and, through Chris, to Ronald—turned out to involve a money-laundering mechanism in Liechtenstein. Ronald and I were both invited to send money that way. Life is too short for deals like this, so both Chris and I had no reservations about turning it down. A year or so later, our host and his mistress were all over the news in Finland: they had been caught by the Finnish government laundering money for Russian oligarchs. Years later, I found out they went to jail for only a couple of days, got out on bond, and then were never prosecuted.

So far, I've mentioned my "success" at deal killing, but there was one occasion on which I fucked up. It's worth describing just how that happened.

A man in Seattle had bought the operating system used by the company Atari. He claimed that the system was so small, it was bound to be the next big thing in cellular phones and wanted Ronald to be his business partner. Ronald asked me to travel with him from New York to Seattle for the meeting. Before we left, Ronald's son-in-law pulled me aside to remind me of my task: "You *must* kill this deal."

We met the man for dinner. It was clear the guy didn't have a penny to his name and likely didn't have his hands on a product destined to become the operating system of the future. So, when the guy stepped away from the table, I told Ronald outright, "Under no circumstances are you going to do this deal."

He agreed.

We returned to the hotel, at which point I made the critical mistake of going to sleep before making sure Ronald went to sleep first. In the morning, as we were about to leave Seattle, I got a phone call from Ronald's office: "Do you know that the guy stayed after and told Ronald his sad life story, and Ronald sent him twenty thousand dollars as a gift?"

There's no question that Ronald Lauder has a big, big heart, but that $20,000 didn't just mar my reputation as a deal killer. It cost me a bit of my well-being, too. For years afterward, the operating system guy would call me regularly, trying to get access to Ronald for more money.

✳

CHAPTER 19

Just before I left RSL, Ruthie and I decided it was time to expand our apartment again. For a couple of years, every time I saw our next-door neighbor, I'd ask him, "When are you selling me your apartment?" At one point, our neighbor told Ruthie that he avoided taking the elevator so that he wouldn't have to hear me repeat the question. The thing was, he was living in a corporate apartment—it wasn't even his own space. To me, it was simple: he was in a position to make some money on the sale, and he could move to an identical apartment just three floors below. Our broker even tried to explain this to him, seemingly to no avail.

Then one day, I received a phone call from our broker. Good news and bad news. The neighbor had decided to sell us the apartment, but he wanted $200,000 above market price. It was more than I imagined he would ask, but I was glad he'd finally understood the value of the deal. He took the money, bought the same apartment on a lower floor, pocketed the $200,000, and Ruthie and I got to expand our place for a second time. With this extension, I added a movie room with a bar and built-in shelves to display some of my collected treasures. The treasures that live in that room are a bit different from the ones I've accumulated elsewhere. There, I placed a collection I'd just started—

comic book hero figurines. Ruthie refers to them as "Itzhak's dolls." I've got all the classics: Superman, Batman, Wolverine, and even a limited edition of Gal Gadot as Wonder Woman. I'd realized as I aged that nearly all of them are characters that had a profound effect on me as a child growing up in Israel. These were heroes who did not cower under threats from their enemies and who always managed to do good in the world. I wanted to feature them prominently in our home.

The same year that we expanded the apartment, it was also time to send Gidi to college. Gidi decidedly liked Tufts University; he was willing to go nowhere else. He applied to only two schools, and at Tufts, he was demoted from the early-admission pool to the regular-admission pool. After that, he was put on the waitlist.

I've mentioned that Gidi is stable, responsible, and extremely charming. Like Ruthie's father, Leo, Gidi will absolutely not like someone, complain about the fact that he has to spend time with them, and then be the most welcoming and generous host they have ever encountered. Knowing his social talents, we called on a connection to arrange some interviews for him with Tufts alumni and donors. Gidi was first interviewed by the rabbi of the campus Hillel and then by a very big New York donor. The afternoon he went for that second interview, it started pouring rain. Gidi had no umbrella with him, so when he arrived at the office of his interviewer, he was sopping wet.

Sopping wet and charming.

The guy fell in love with him, put in a good word, and Gidi got plucked off the waitlist along with very few others. When his acceptance letter arrived, Ruthie and I were convinced that this was a big miracle. That's when Gidi waved the acceptance letter at us and said with great confidence, "You see?"

Now, when Ruthie went to college, her parents dropped her off there and never returned. Celia and Leo were always happy with how well Ruthie did in school, but they were not paying attention to any of the details. With Gidi, Ruthie and I decided to visit during Parents and Family Weekend, an event that occurred only a handful of weeks after we'd dropped him off. He was still adjusting to the scene at college, and we felt tremendously sad that he was away from us.

We dealt with our feelings by undertaking major renovations to the apartment. For eight months, Ruthie, Chooby, and I had no kitchen. Ruthie refused to let the workers disconnect our refrigerator, so it stood in the center of a wall-less space with one functional electrical wire leading to it. We ate in the bathroom, we tiptoed around scattered-about building materials, and we argued about design choices right up until I gave Ruthie complete control over the matter.

When I left Ronald's offices in 2002 after finishing the period during which my RSL severance was paid out, Ruthie found me an office in Carnegie Hall Tower. I worked out of that office for another five years, evaluating opportunities and investing in several of them.

I should say that not all the business investments Ruthie and I made during that period were successful. And I certainly hadn't had much luck with earlier attempts. Back in our twenties, I'd invested $100,000 in the best-looking horse ranch in all of Israel. The lesson I learned was a simple one: don't invest in businesses you know nothing about. Feeding the horses alone costs a tremendous amount of money. I lost the entire investment. Then, a decade later, Ronald and I invested in a project to build a megacasino in Hungary. We had met with the relevant ministers, and everything seemed to be going well. But then Viktor Orbán was elected prime minister, and he deemed the whole project a bad idea. There would be no casino. The lesson there? Even deals that seem to be going well can be derailed by unpredictable factors. The way I've come to think of investing since then is that in high-risk, high-reward scenarios, you have to know how to lose money. If you cannot handle losing your investment, you should not be involved in the deal.

Over the years, and the more we practiced, Ruthie and I got better at telling good entrepreneurs from bad ones, unicorn ideas from their more promising counterparts. Usually, if one out of every ten investments does well, it makes up for the rest; we were lucky to have a much better ratio. We invested in a successful ad-tech company, an online therapy company, a computer software company, a watch company—projects like these counteracted losses from other investments enough to benefit us overall.

In 2002, we met a young man named Ori, whom I still refer to as the "crazy scientist." His idea would propel one of the biggest transitions in social media analytics. He was the son of a friend in Israel, and he came in to pitch a start-up company named Trendum that analyzed people's real-time social media feedback on television shows. I'll admit that when he came to talk with me, I liked the concept but found him so unfocused that I couldn't concentrate enough to make sense of everything he was saying.

So, I sent him to Ruthie.

Even she noticed that he struggled to concentrate on his own presentation, but she, too, liked his idea. And then came the somewhat inexplicable part of these meetings where she liked the idea enough to believe we should support him.

"Have you ever watched the show *Six Feet Under*?" he asked her. Then, without giving her an opportunity to respond, he continued: "I did an analysis of the show, and here's what I learned ..."

Ruthie had not yet watched the show, but she was very impressed with the detailed conclusions he had drawn. *What do I know?* she thought to herself. *Sure!*

Before committing fully to supporting his project, I brought our scientist to talk with executives at HBO. He presented a deep dive into a couple of episodes of the show *Carnival,* pointing out what people liked about the storyline and its characters. It was a fascinating two-hour meeting, during which the excitement in the room grew steadily. At the end, the kid asked the execs, "Could you please give me a couple of episodes to watch? I've never seen the show."

That was the moment when I agreed that Ruthie and I would invest in his company. I became Trendum's executive chair and devoted quite a bit of my time to its development.

Then, in March 2003, what we call Gulf War II, or the Israel–Iraq War, occurred. I was worried enough about my parents that we moved them from Tel Aviv to Miami for a month—nearly the entirety of the war—and they lived in an apartment complex where my uncles owned property. As expected, my father loved being there and spent most of his time lounging in or by the pool and talking with the other residents. My mother spent nearly all her time inside the apartment.

In some ways, the way they approached Miami was not unlike the way things were when they traveled to see us in New York—my mother liked being in the apartment; my father liked spending all day talking with Ruthie's father and uncle about their histories and enjoying the city's energy. Even during the last decade of his life, when he was deteriorating from Parkinson's disease, he'd be so happy taking walks down New York streets with Ruthie and breathing in what he joked was the city's "delicious air." He'd tear up and throw his cane into the street, saying that he didn't need it anymore, because New York made every bit of life so enjoyable. The older he got, the weepier he got, but we always showed him a good time when he was here. The less capable he became of traveling, the more efforts I made to visit

Israel regularly—and even more regularly in his last couple of years, when he couldn't move much at all.

Gidi did well in school and started a serious relationship with a fellow student named Nina in the spring semester of his senior year in college. We'd all heard quite a bit about Nina, and the family was excited to meet her during graduation weekend. But Gidi and Nina broke up the night before we all arrived. Ruthie and I did our best to let everyone know what had happened before we all gathered for dinner, but by then Ruthie's father, Leo, had started to suffer the effects of Alzheimer's disease. "My brain isn't working right," he'd pointed out earlier that year. When it came time to celebrate Gidi's achievement over a big family meal, Leo couldn't keep from asking over and over again, "Where's the girlfriend?" Ruthie's mother would tell him in Polish to keep quiet, but it didn't help. "Where's the girl?" he asked about every ten minutes.

Not long after he graduated, I brought Gidi into the start-up environment at Trendum as employee number two in the US doing sales and marketing. He was thinking about entering a big corporate environment, but he also had a strong interest in doing something more entrepreneurial. Gidi quickly revealed a talent for liaising between customers and the technology operation in Israel. Our customers would indicate how they wanted the product to work, and Gidi would help the tech team understand and prioritize those needs to elevate the product overall. He was good at breaking through the stubbornness of the technology team, telling them again and again that these were customers who knew their business needs well and really did need to be taken seriously.

Trendum was a true "seat of the pants" start-up environment, and Gidi and Rich Nelson—his boss and employee number one in the US—would go out to give presentations without having all the materials they needed. Neither of them found this amusing. For any number of big pitches, Gidi or Rich might find himself running into a meeting, screaming into the phone, "You need to send me the presentation right now!"

As a lawyer, Rich was used to overpreparing, but there they'd be, he and Gidi, arriving late to a meeting, sweating, and then presenting slides they hadn't yet seen, not knowing what the next one might show. Rich always claimed that he didn't handle stress well, but I think getting the slides at the last moment allowed him to develop a skill that helped him in the long run, maybe even in life in general.

The reason they were always scrambling for material is that the systems we were using at the time spit out unrefined data. There was no AI or other sophisticated analytic instrument, which meant we needed to rely on a bunch of analysts to wrangle data and then put it into presentation format. They always delivered at the last minute.

On my end, there were some interesting developments when it came to raising money from Israeli funds. It was a little like the Wild West—lawless and risky. When we did a road show offering 20 percent of the company for $5 million, I learned that Israeli funds are very aggressive when it comes to valuation. They would tell me, "Here is five million for twenty percent, but we want you to assign twenty percent to future management team hires that are not going to dilute us." So, in fact, we would have received $5 million, but that would get diluted by 40 percent—20 percent to them and 20 percent to the management team. I found the whole thing off putting.

Then, an uncomfortable situation arose when two competing funds became interested in Trendum.

As I was telling Fred Langhammer about all this back-and-forth between the two funds, he suggested that Nielsen—a global leader in audience measurement—might be the best home for Trendum.

He was going to golf with Nielsen's CEO and offered to mention our situation.

That sounded great to me!

Nielsen's CEO was very interested and set a meeting for the following day. When I arrived, I was introduced to a guy in charge of mergers and acquisitions. I knew from this detail alone that he had been told to do a deal, which was an absolutely great situation for Trendum to be in. I offered the 20 percent for $5 million arrangement, and he agreed. Then he asked for Nielsen to have preferred shares, which meant that if Trendum were to be sold, Nielsen would get its money first. This is a very common ask, but because I knew he didn't have a choice—I was meeting with him because he'd been told to do a deal—my answer was "Absolutely not!"

He agreed.

It was important to me to maintain an excellent relationship with both of the Israeli funds, and I was able to turn both down without causing any friction. When it comes to finding a strategic partner, there's no argument to be made. In the entirety of my professional career, whenever I have raised money from venture funds, reassurance is always given about their very healthy Rolodex of potential clients, potential hires, and potential additional investors. But in nearly every instance, a venture fund is going to be a financial partner and not much of a strategic helper. Venture funds are primarily concerned with the numbers. When it comes to strategic partnerships, numbers are important, but the product and its appeal to clients are much more important. It's just so much healthier for a company to align with a strategic partner.

From the deal, Nielsen got 20 percent of the company, a seat on the board, and a bird's-eye view into how Israelis were doing business at the time.

Next, I turned my attention to buying Trendum's two primary competitors: IntelliSeek, the bigger operator in the field, and Buzz-Metrics. We made a deal with BuzzMetrics and then asked Nielsen for a $20 million loan to help us acquire IntelliSeek.

When it came to purchasing IntelliSeek, the situation was more complicated. This was the problem in a nutshell: IntelliSeek had more than thirty shareholders, all of whom attended the meeting with me, and all of whom seemed unwilling to budge in negotiations. I learned that Nielsen had looked at IntelliSeek before they looked at us but then decided against purchasing them precisely because of all the shareholder engagement.

We held the deal-negotiation meeting in a big boardroom at Nielsen. No one person was authorized to speak on behalf of the entire group; potentially, they might all have pushed in different directions.

"I would like to offer you twenty million dollars," I began.

They were united in responding, "We want fifty."

"You are not going to get fifty. I'll offer you twenty-five million dollars."

"No, fifty."

I saw that I would never be able to negotiate with them.

In negotiations, the respective parties expect one another to move. I showed them that I would move. They showed me that they would not. I imagined them having agreed on only one thing beforehand: "Nielsen has deep pockets, so we're going to hold still on our agreed-upon number until we get it."

I tried a different approach.

"Listen, at twenty, you didn't move; at twenty-five, you didn't move. I know that you will never move, and there's no lead person in this room for me to talk to. This is my final offer: thirty million dollars and one seat on the board. I'm leaving the room."

"What is happening?"

"How can you say final offer?"

"Don't leave the room!"

They were all yelling at once.

"You have the conference room until five o'clock." I pointed through the glass. "I'm going to go to my office, which is right over there. If there is a deal, send someone to my office and let me know. If not, you can leave; you don't have to say goodbye."

"You cannot leave!" A few of them rushed to block the door.

"I'm out!" And I exited the room.

The Nielsen guy who left with me started laughing his head off as soon as we were safely out of earshot.

It was a bit past eleven in the morning. For the rest of the day, anyone who walked past that conference room could have a good look at thirty stressed-out people pacing back and forth, waving their arms, and occasionally screaming at one another.

At exactly 5:00 p.m., they sent Mahendra, the founder, to my office. "You have a deal."

They had all chosen Mahendra to hold the board position.

I did the deals with BuzzMetrics and IntelliSeek without telling either of them about our intended acquisition of the other. After the IntelliSeek deal went through, I got to deliver the news to both companies at once: "We accomplished deals with both of you, and we're combining all three entities into one company."

We merged the platforms and took the BuzzMetrics name. The CEO of IntelliSeek became the CEO of the combined company, the CEO of Trendum became head of product, and the CEO of BuzzMetrics became head of international. And that's how we turned Trendum into the largest social media analytics company at that time.

My fondest memory of the board meetings that followed was approving the minutes from the prior meeting. Every single time, Mahendra would raise his hand and go into an extended speech about all the issues he had with the minutes.

"I said it this way, not that way. I suggest that we do this and this." And on he would go.

As I saw it, he was a minority shareholder focused on details having to do only with his opinions. I wanted us all to be working together on the big picture: building a successful company. So, every time Mahendra finished his speech, I would turn to the secretary of our board and our company lawyer and say, "Rich, please note in the minutes that Mahendra registered all his objections. The chairman has noted all of Mahendra's comments and objections and rejected them all. Now, let's continue."

That was our ritual at the start of every meeting. Mahendra never quit.

Two representatives from Nielsen attended the meetings, and the first few times I made this gesture, I could see that they were horrified by my approach. They didn't know what to do. But eventually they laughed out loud. When a company is performing well, those in charge can push things along the way they want and, as Mahendra helped me prove, without much fuss.

CHAPTER 20

I t took Chooby until his final two years of high school before he got competitive about his grades, and then he ended up graduating second in his class. Before then, he didn't care about any of it. When it came time for him to go to college, Ruthie and I knew we would have to be clever. Our second son had developed into quite a contrarian. If we liked something, he inevitably hated it. If we recommended something, he was sure to do the opposite.

Chooby started college the year Gidi graduated college. During Gidi's four years at Tufts, Ruthie and I joined the Parents Leadership Council and became its cochairs (which of course meant that Ruthie was fully in charge). She liked Tufts, and she liked her role helping to raise money for the school; we both really wanted Chooby to choose it.

To that end, we encouraged him to go elsewhere.

Ruthie took him on a special trip to her alma mater, Johns Hopkins, and even turned to him at one point and said outright, "Your father and I would be very happy if you went to school here." When he chose Tufts, we high-fived behind his back!

In his first week at Tufts, he hosted a twenty-person beer pong party in his room and received a disciplinary warning. Two weeks later, in his haste to hide his bong before answering a knock at the door, the bong fell to the floor and shattered. Chooby was suspended temporarily and restricted from joining a fraternity that year. Of course, he joined his chosen fraternity unofficially.

When he told me about the incident that got him suspended, I didn't understand what he was talking about. So I called Gidi and asked, "What is a bong? Is it serious drugs?" To this day, they both poke fun at me for not knowing.

In his sophomore year in college, Chooby heard from the Hillel rabbi at Tufts about a Hebrew tribe, the Abayudaya, living in rural Uganda, west of Entebbe. Chooby decided he wanted to visit the tribe for a month, so he came up with a project to collect used personal computers, bring them to the tribe, and help the people there learn how to use them. He, Ruthie, and I had several talks and a few fights over his interest in making the trip. At the time, we didn't know terribly much about the entire continent of Africa, and we would have preferred him to choose a city location rather than one far from resources he might need while there. In the end, Chooby found a way to do what he wanted, and he even took a friend along with him.

How did he manage to convince us that he should make the trip?

He made a case that I could not deny. The November before he asked to spend time in Uganda, he came out to me and Ruthie. It was the eve of our twenty-fifth wedding anniversary when he said to us, "I think I'm gay." That lack of definitiveness in speech, the *I think* at the start of his revelation, is what caught my attention. I had been shocked by his words—shaken by them, even. So, I focused on the *I think* as if the phrase hinted that Chooby was not yet sure.

When about four months later we argued with him about visiting the Ugandan tribe, he made the case that traveling to a rural town in Africa to connect with African Jews would help him clear his head. I imagined that this could be the experience that would help change his mind about his sexual orientation.

We joke about "handling" Chooby, about the subtle or not-so-subtle ways we have discovered for influencing his decisions. But just as much, he has "handled" us—known enough about our desires to turn them in his favor. Though there have been times when he's chosen a path I haven't understood, Chooby is, and always has been, the child most like me and Gidi the one most like Ruthie. There's no denying the similarities.

Chooby had been in Uganda nearly a month when we agreed that he would leave and meet up with me and Gidi in Germany at that year's World Cup game. Prior to his arrival in Munich, Chooby had displayed a real knack for losing everything that we bought for him. As a kid, he lost a new bike as well as a series of new winter coats, and after that we mostly stopped keeping track. But to my amazement, he showed up in Munich with every article of clothing he had taken with him to Uganda. And every article of clothing he had with him was torn, dirty, and full of holes.

I'd wanted to treat the boys, so I got them a big hotel suite and booked myself a small separate room. Gidi and I were both standing there in the suite when Chooby, on his way to the shower, took off his shirt to reveal a chest full of pock marks. Though no one in Uganda sleeps on the floor, Chooby did. That's how he ended up with maggots all over his torso. The people there had helped him rid himself of the maggots by burning them off. As a result, Chooby's torso was covered with burned indentations where maggots had once tried to make their home.

He wasn't fazed. But in that moment, Gidi and I insisted, "Throw away all the clothes!"

I still have a drawer full of used personal computers—Chooby collected more than he needed to take with him on his travels. That said, Chooby did develop a love for Uganda—and, as we continue to discover, for more countries in Africa—and he continued to pursue his own creative business ideas from that point forward. Before he graduated college, he started a business called Breakfast Alarm—an early version of a food-delivery app—by developing relationships with all the restaurants around Tufts so that students could order online after a late night out and have breakfast delivered to them in their dorm rooms.

When it came to revealing the effects of his trip, he waited almost another full year before revisiting the topic of needing to clear his head. This time, it was the night before we were to travel to San Diego for four weeks; we planned to grieve with our friends there who had lost their son in a hiking accident. And this time, Chooby was certain that he was gay.

I have to credit Chooby for having impeccable timing.

While Chooby was busy finishing his international relations degree at Tufts, Gidi earned a promotion within BuzzMetrics and became head of mobile product.

I've mentioned that Nielsen initially owned 20 percent of the company called Trendum, which, when we acquired and combined companies, took the name BuzzMetrics. Back when Nielsen made its initial investment, it was a public company with a Dutch management team. Within a half year or so of their investing in 20 percent of our company, that team tried to merge Nielsen with another company and agreed to a deal where they would give the other company's management full control. There was a shareholder revolt at Nielsen. The deal did not happen, share prices plummeted, and private equity stepped in and bought the company. When they did, they hired Dave Calhoun from General Electric to be the new CEO.

In my first meeting with Dave, he asked me, "What do you think about Nielsen?"

Having inherited from my mother the inclination to say exactly what I think, I answered, "The company sucks."

"Why?"

I started listing problems. "The structure is too complex. There are too many people doing the same jobs. Your whole management team is full of yes-people, so you never get a straight answer when you talk with anyone. People are generally unavailable. There is zero innovation ..."

Instead of dismissing me with a firm handshake and a quick end to the conversation, Dave invited me to attend an off-site meeting in Miami, his first, with Nielsen's top 250 team members. There were two aspects of that gathering at which I almost laughed out loud— once in shock, and once in recognition of something I already knew. First, at the initial reception I witnessed all 250 people exchanging business cards with one another. I was blown away by the fact that so many of them seemed to be meeting each other for the first time. And second, during the more structured meetings, one of two things kept occurring—either Dave would make an observation and everyone would agree with it, or Dave would ask a question and everyone would jump at the chance to see if they could say what they believed he wanted to hear.

In that context, you might wonder what made my relationship with Dave work so well. The thing was, he loved that I was an independent thinker and more than willing to say exactly what I thought.

Still, it surprised me when he asked to meet for dinner and proposed that Nielsen buy BuzzMetrics outright and that I come work for him as part of Nielsen's senior management team.

I'd been doing business on my own for so long and found it so enjoyable that the idea of entering a big corporate environment really did not appeal to me. So, I made sure to reiterate to Dave those aspects of my personality that might not work so well for him in the long term. "I'm not sure you want me in a big company. The fact that I always say what I think could create a lot of issues …"

"To the contrary," he countered. "I absolutely need someone who is willing to do just that. And if your approach is a little bit like being a bull in a china shop … well, at least you'll be *my* bull."

I was free and didn't want to give up being free, but I was intrigued by Dave's offer. He would make me one of the top executives in the company and allow me 25 percent of my time to work on my own projects. Dave made it seem like it couldn't hurt to give the arrangement a try.

"There is only one condition," I insisted.

"What's that?"

"My wife has to agree."

"Okaaaay."

"And she's not that far away. Let me call her."

Ruthie took a cab and joined us at our restaurant table. The three of us had a conversation, and so began the acquisition of BuzzMetrics and my time spent as a Nielsen executive, a role I stayed in for seven years. That's as long as I stayed at Aurec, the Israeli company that had felt like my first home.

The BuzzMetrics acquisition was amusing, because it involved Tom Mastrelli, who had negotiated the deal with me back when Nielsen purchased 20 percent of Trendum. I've mentioned that one of the things I learned early on about negotiating is to find out as much as possible about whom I'm negotiating with and then use that knowledge as a way of establishing trust and guiding the conversation.

With Tom, I'd learned that if I didn't say much of anything, he would negotiate with himself for an hour or more and then end up offering me the best possible deal. So, when it came time for Nielsen to own 100 percent of BuzzMetrics, not only did Tom propose matching the valuation from the accreditor; he forgave us the debt we were carrying rather than deducting it from the purchase price. What that means is that Tom decided—without any intervention from me—to give us more than the company's valuation amount! And all I had to do was stay quiet while he went through the paperwork and discussed each step: "Let's see, we can do this here, and it would work like this. And then, come to think about it, this and this ..."

In the end, it was the best deal ever.

In my new role at Nielsen, I became Tom's boss. In my opinion, he had one quality that nobody could match—he'd been with the company for a long time and knew all the ins and outs. So, I kept him as my historian, and we had a productive working relationship even after he eventually left the company.

Dave built a strong management team. He gave us a lot of rope, as the saying goes, so each of us had the freedom to operate as we saw fit. As I saw it, there was just one exception to that general rule—an exception that I found both interesting and, at least initially, challenging. To my surprise, Dave spent over 50 percent of his time on HR matters. He'd brought with him from General Electric a system that had become popular there: you rank your people every quarter and then fire the bottom 10 percent at the close of every year. What worked about this system was that every employee knew where they stood, and everyone had clear targets to reach in order to improve. In the beginning, I didn't buy into the system, and I struggled to rank people. The first time I tried, I put everyone somewhere in the middle of the grid. The only person I put in the lowest 10 percent was a guy I had already fired.

Then I showed my work to Dave. "Typical!" he said, laughing.

I ended up needing specific guidance from HR about how to make meaningful distinctions about people's performance, leadership, and so on. Once I got good at it, I became invested in the simplicity and clarity of the method.

One year into my employment at Nielsen, it was time for another off-site meeting. I suggested to Dave that we run a competition among all forty thousand employees for product ideas. The top five idea holders would earn the chance to present to the top 250 employees, and Nielsen would pledge to create the winning product.

It was a big success. The best ideas ended up coming from five people who would otherwise never have had the opportunity to spend time with the top 250. We held that competition annually until the year I left the company, and every time, we turned the winning idea into a new product. Many times, we turned the top three ideas into products—they were that good.

When we sold BuzzMetrics to Nielsen, Gidi made some good money from the shares he owned. He also transferred over to Nielsen along with me and stayed there for four years doing corporate development work before striking out on his own. In 2012, he developed an e-commerce start-up that combined price tracking and coupon validation. That project went far—he grew the company to a million users—but his revenue model wasn't sustainable, and he decided to shutter the platform. His primary competitor was also not successful, but that competitor kept his company alive on a string while he went and found himself another job. Eventually, the product caught fire, and the competitor sold his company for $1 billion. It took Gidi a while to recover from having an idea that didn't catch on until after he let go of it. The good news was that Nina was back in his life, and we all finally got to meet her. We fell in love with her and were thrilled that he was dating a wonderful, smart, and very pretty girl.

While Gidi was growing bored at a big company like Nielsen, Chooby was busy seeking excitement at every turn. He graduated from Tufts in 2008 and decided that he wanted to enlist in the Israeli army. You might guess that Ruthie and I were not thrilled with this idea and that Chooby didn't take no for an answer. After his first day assigned to the infantry, he called us, hysterical: "I don't care if I go to jail! I need to get out of here!" I utilized my connections to arrange for him to work in the spokesperson unit. While there, he made great friends, created new digital channels for the army, and worked on his own start-up venture helping people find and meet up at local events and parties.

When he returned home after two years of service, we gave him some weeks to adjust and then let him know that he needed to find work and a place to live. I offered to help him out, but he insisted that he would find employment on his own. He applied for a lot of jobs but got zero interviews. Why? Because Chooby was applying only to senior management positions like CEO of Google. He was getting no bites, but he wanted to show us that he was serious about working, so he went out one afternoon and got himself some work as a runner in a nearby restaurant. If I remember right, he worked there for about a month before he quit.

One afternoon not long thereafter, he dropped by my office at Nielsen for a visit. The head of operations was sitting with me when Chooby came in. I introduced them, and about five minutes later, Chooby had a job offer in operations. I wasn't sure that Nielsen was the right environment for Chooby, but as it turned out, he loved it! And he did a great job. He and the daughter of the head of operations worked as a team, innovating together. They started measuring the most-watched shows on streaming video; before any competitor, they were reporting how many hours US consumers spent on Netflix, Hulu, and the rest. The initiative caught a lot of press. It was fun for them to do, and Nielsen's reputation was enhanced by their work.

If I had to guess, I'd say that what Chooby liked most about his time at Nielsen was working on a very small team, detached from most everyone else in the company, with nobody telling him what to do. When eventually that situation changed, he would have to leave in order to more directly indulge his entrepreneurial tendencies.

CHAPTER 21

Leo's dementia continued to progress during the five years leading up to his passing, and all the while Celia refused to let anyone help her take care of him. Ruthie arranged for caregivers to appear at their house on the regular, but each new person wouldn't survive a full twenty-four hours before being summarily fired by Celia. So, Ruthie decided that we would move both her parents into the city; this way, she could check in on them more frequently. Because the move was Ruthie's decision and not theirs, Ruthie was also the one who had to make all the arrangements. Her mother refused to participate in any of the decision-making.

Then, Leo died a week before the movers were set to pack up all their belongings in Great Neck and shuttle them to Manhattan.

When Ruthie finally moved her mother out of the house in Great Neck, her mother still refused to participate in the process, choosing instead to sit in a chair and look on silently as the house was packed and loaded onto the moving truck. When it was finally time to clear out of the house, Ruthie approached her mother. "We're all packed, and we're going now. If you want to stay here, you stay here. But we're going to the city."

Not until that moment did her mother agree to the move. "Okay," she said, with a sigh of deep resignation. "I'm going to the city."

Ruthie looked on as Celia walked into her bathroom, picked up two items—her toothbrush and her hair spray—shoved them into her handbag, and returned to Ruthie's side. That was all the packing she would do before leaving her house forever.

My father's death from Parkinson's disease followed within a year of Leo's passing. My mother took care of him with the help of an aide, and I flew to Israel several times a year to check in on them both. The last time I saw my father alive, I knew it would be our final visit. By then, he was mostly unable to move, but when I stood up to leave his bedside, his hand reached out to cover mine, and he held me tightly.

After my father passed, I stayed in Israel for a couple of weeks. I've mentioned before that my mother was a hoarder of food, but the older she got, the other thing she had started hoarding was pills. She had a pill for everything. And the pills, as if on display, covered the entire dining room table. To keep track of her collection, she had a designated pill box for each day of the week. The more time I spent with her, the more I noticed just how much time she spent organizing and managing her pills.

When I took her for a checkup with her doctor, she didn't say a word throughout the entire thing. The doctor talked on and on, and then, it seemed, the visit was over. That's when Haviva leaned in and said to him, "Doctor, can I have some pills?"

"Well, you know, maybe this … and this …" He started making suggestions.

"I have all of those already," she answered him. "Do you have anything *else*?"

I witnessed as they back and forth for a bit. Every pill he offered, she had it already.

I decided it would be good for my mother to visit me and Ruthie for a while, so we brought her to stay with us in New York for a month, and we had a very good time together. Granted, she managed to make some mischief while she was there. She would sneak into one of our windowless bathrooms to smoke cigarettes, and inevitably she would set the smoke detector blaring.

I'd arrive to resolve the issue, and each time she'd ask me, "Why is this alarm going off?"

"Ma," I'd announce, "you smoked!"

"I smoked?" she'd shoot back, looking as innocent as a child.

Though Ruthie's mother had resisted moving into the city, she had a wonderful life once she did. We got her an apartment just two blocks from ours. She made new friends, she played bridge regularly, she had dinners with us and the kids on Fridays, and she stayed involved with her neighborhood and community for twelve years.

Haviva, by contrast, did not do well at all. She was nine years younger than Martin and only eighty years old, but she died just a year after he did and within a week of the day he passed. Even with all her pills, the shock of losing my father was more than she could bear.

Leo's and Martin's deaths were both a long time coming. Even though they occurred within a remarkably short period of time, their gradual demise had prepared us, at least in part, for their passing. But my mother's death was a surprise. She seemed to have known it would arrive sooner than later, because when she visited us in New York City, she spoke almost prophetically: "This is the end. I will never be able to visit you again." Her deterioration from that point on was sharp and quick. When she returned to Tel Aviv, she asked to be moved into an assisted-living facility near my sister. Just after settling in, she went over to the common dining room for dinner. She called me afterward to summarize, "I'm not going back over there. It's all old people!"

Not long thereafter, she was in and out of the hospital—her emphysema worsening from persistent smoking, her deteriorating bones making it a struggle just to walk. And then, she was gone.

When you bring all your family together for Passover, one of the rituals involves remembering all the Passovers up until the present one. When I started participating as a child, my grandfather was the head of the table; later, it was my parents, and then in the US, it was Ruthie's father and all her family. Then Ruthie and I took over responsibility for the Seder. We are now on the front line. We don't want to be on the front line, mind you. We would prefer to hide behind our elders. But here we are, in charge, so to speak. One day, it will be someone else.

When you are the youngest kid at the table, you sing the question song, "Ma Nishtana." When someone else is born after you, that child sings the song, and then you progress through the years until at some point you have moved on from being the youngest to being the head of the Seder. And then you're gone. As head of the table, you enjoy being surrounded by your nearest and dearest, but you think, too, about the legacy you will leave and the way you'll be remembered by those who come after you.

There might have been some questions in the back of my mind about what I would leave behind, but in the time following the deaths of three of our parents, I focused on what I had to give.

And I started that giving at Nielsen. The company had a small Israeli operation—a few hundred people out of nearly forty thousand employees in total. Given my connections within the country, I suggested to Dave that we visit Nielsen's Israeli arm and then tour the country together. Dave jumped at the opportunity, so I arranged a series of visits to historical locations and meetings for him—as well as our company's COO and CFO—to talk with Israeli businesspeople and politicians. I wanted them to have a visit they would remember always. Among others, they met with the finance minister and the ministers of education and culture, and then I took them for dinner to the home of the defense minister. The coup de grâce was a meeting with Bibi himself, who had once again been elected the country's prime minister.

I'd called well before we left the US to arrange that meeting with Bibi. Then, just one day before it was to take place, I received notice that it would be delayed by an hour. Then, an hour after that, I received notice that it was delayed again. Those calls kept coming throughout the day, all the way until 7:00 p.m., at which point the meeting was officially canceled. Bibi's chief of staff telephoned to say as much.

"Listen," I replied. "This meeting is very important to me. I scheduled it from the US well before we even made the trip here. All day long, you've been moving the time, and now you are canceling outright. Tell Bibi that he and I are done."

Not ten minutes later, I received a call from Bibi himself. "Itzhak! Nobody told me the meeting is supposed to be with *you*. But you should know I can only do half an hour."

"That's perfectly fine. You should know that you're meeting the head of Nielsen, who, by the way, was also the number two person at General Electric."

"Of course!"

The next day, we gathered in the conference room at a Tel Aviv hotel. The conversation got underway with Bibi and Dave talking about the projects General Electric used to do in Israel, and I could see they were feeding off each other's charisma.

Forty-five minutes into the "thirty-minute" meeting, Bibi asked the servers, "Do you have any food for us?"

Within minutes, the entire table was filled with food—there wasn't even room for people to rest their plates. To this day, Dave reminds me that he never saw so much food in his life. Our thirty-minute meeting turned into a three-hour meeting in which everyone attending had a great time. The connections Dave made that day and throughout that trip continued to serve well all the companies he worked for.

I also made sure to take Dave on a tour of Jerusalem. That was my first time visiting the Christian area of Jerusalem and the locations designated as the sites of the last supper, crucifixion, and burial. There is a particular slab of marble where it is said Jesus's body was rested after the crucifixion; everyone is drawn to touch it. When we arrived at the site, Dave got on his knees to touch the stone, tears in his eyes. I didn't know Dave to be a deeply religious man, so I asked, "Why did you become so emotional here?"

"It got to me. I've met the pope twice. But meeting the pope and visiting the Vatican is nothing like being present in the place where history happened and walking in the footsteps of Jesus."

In my mind, it was worth bringing him to Israel just for that—to have an experience he would never forget.

What I didn't anticipate was that after we returned from that trip, a lot of talk circulated within the company about my political and business connections in Israel. It didn't help that Dave began treating me as if I were the master of everything related to Israel, capable of making anything happen there. As is my nature, I decided to lean into everyone's perceptions and suspicions. If we were in a management meeting and talking about our competitors, I would look over at Dave with a straight face and say something like, "Dave, would you like me to take them out?"

Neither of us would break character, but both of us would enjoy the silence that temporarily consumed the entire room.

The only time that my "leaning in" caused me some distress was when there was actual business Nielsen was vying for in Israel. The country was running a competition to replace a participant in its incubator incentive program—an innovation-boosting endeavor in which the winning company contributes 10 percent of the funds for its start-up ideas and the Israeli government contributes the remaining 90 percent. If a start-up succeeded, the government would get its money back, plus interest. If a start-up failed, the government and the company would both lose out.

The incubator program got its start back in the 1970s when there was an influx of Russian immigrants who were engineers. Israel didn't have many employment opportunities for them, but the country believed it needed to find a way to provide them with meaningful work. When that program proved successful, the government opened it up to competitors of all kinds. That shift significantly boosted the start-up scene throughout the country.

Israel offers about ten licenses, each of ten-year duration, to participants in the incubator program, and every three or four years one of those licenses becomes available. There is, as you might imagine, lots of competition for that one spot in the program. Hundreds of companies apply for the one license. When Dave encouraged us to apply, our main competitor was Elbit, a multibillion-dollar weapons and technology company. I went to Dave to express my concern about competing with Elbit. Dave just looked at me and said, "Itzhak, there's no way you won't get the license. I saw you! You have the whole government of Israel in your pocket!"

I of course did the requisite lobbying, but I also couldn't help but think, *What the hell have I done?*

I was a wreck as we waited to hear which company secured the license. When we won it, I called Dave, both thrilled and thoroughly relieved.

"Of course you got it!" was all he said in response.

During the period in which Nielsen held the license, it made between twenty-five and thirty investments in businesses focused on marketing, consumer, and advertising research technologies. Winning the license was a highlight for me, because Nielsen is now doing serious business in Israel investing in the start-up ecosystem there.

I would be remiss not to mention other highlights of my time spent creating trouble for myself while working for Dave. So, I'll tell you about how, at another of the off-site gatherings, Dave invited me to play table tennis with him in front of everyone. He knew I had developed an avid attachment to the game around the time I started working for Nielsen.

"You don't want to do this, Dave," I said in response. "I don't throw games."

"No, no. I want you to play."

When our meetings finished on the afternoon of our match, I went to my room and got suited up for the game. I put on my shorts, my T-shirt, my tennis shoes. When I arrived in the lobby, I noticed that Dave was still dressed as before, wearing his suit trousers and his dress shirt.

We played three games. The scores were 21–5, 21–4, and 21–3. I crushed him.

Our HR leader pulled me aside. "That was a very bad career move," he started.

"What career?" I answered.

The next day, Dave made an announcement to the group. "As you saw yesterday, I played table tennis with Itzhak. He came with his table tennis shoes, with his table tennis outfit, with his racquet that probably cost a lot of money, and he beat the shit out of me. I'll tell you the truth—I was okay with it. I didn't care … until I came home and told my kids. They really gave me a tough time."

Thankfully, playing table tennis didn't always get me into trouble at Nielsen. On occasion, it yielded opportunities to make lucrative deals. On one of my trips to China, for example, the consultant working for us said that she could introduce me to Zhuang Zedong, the world champion of table tennis in the early 1970s. By the time I met him, of course, he was in his seventies. We went to his house, played a match, and he killed me. It was an amazing experience. Seeing how much I appreciated playing, our consultant later took me to a club where businesspeople play on the regular.

I went in, played against a guy I didn't know, and won. That's when we introduced ourselves to one another. I learned that he was the head of the Chinese census bureau; he learned that I was from Nielsen. He suggested that we work on a joint product for the consumer confidence index of China. I agreed and handed things over to our head of operations in China. Within eight months, we'd done a deal with the Chinese census bureau, and I was invited back to the country. Given that we were the two people who'd gotten the project started, the head of the bureau insisted that I attend the deal signing.

Then, he also insisted that we play a table tennis game in front of everybody.

This time, it was Nielsen's head of operations in China who pulled me aside before the match: "Itzhak, you *must* lose."

"I don't throw table tennis games."

"Are you crazy? It's the consumer confidence index. This is a big breakthrough for Nielsen in China, and you're going to win in front of all this guy's employees?"

"I don't throw any games."

"What the hell are you doing? I'm going to call Dave."

"Okay. But I am not throwing the game."

We played the first game, and I won. I looked over at the head of operations, who was white as a sheet, completely beside himself.

And then we played a second game. Fair and square, my competitor won.

And that was when the head of operations leaped out of his chair and announced, "This is an absolutely perfect time to stop!"

The group was delighted. Including me.

✤

CHAPTER 22

lthough I didn't initially want to work in a big company
like Nielsen, I enjoyed myself the entire time I was there.
If I chose to, I could invest in any project that came to
Nielsen in a nascent stage. And during that time, Ruthie
and I also pursued other investment opportunities apart from what
Nielsen had to offer. For the first five years that I worked at Nielsen, I
was head of global product, with about ten thousand people reporting
to me. Then, in 2012, Dave took the company public again, which
put Nielsen's capacity to increase profits back in the spotlight. Just one
day before the 2012 off-site meeting, Dave informed me that he was
taking away my job responsibilities, distributing them across multiple
units within the company, and giving me a new set of responsibilities
as executive vice president for global business development. I would
be responsible for strategic initiatives and mergers and acquisitions. I
wasn't sure how I felt about that.

Before I had time to respond, he announced the change in
my title and responsibilities to everyone at the off-site meeting. It
was a clever move—and one that ultimately won me over. And it
was this new position that made deal making and negotiation the
primary focus of my job. I'd been negotiating deals all the while that

I'd developed expertise in data and analytics, but I was not heading negotiations until receiving this particular promotion.

I relished the opportunity to perfect my skills and kept paying better and closer attention to the people with whom I was engaged in deal making. My ability to do that grew much subtler and less overt. I took even more time to understand people simply by interacting with them, getting to know them far beyond whatever information was available to me before any meeting.

I have so many stories to tell about making deals during my time at Nielsen, and frankly I've been tempted to include even more than the few featured here. But Ruthie keeps reminding me that no one needs to read about all the different negotiations. She might be right; she usually is. But for me, each experience was unique, utterly dependent on specific people and their motivations, on circumstances and timing, on the mood around the negotiating table. For every element of sense making and predictability in the numbers and the paperwork, some downright nonsense and unpredictability could lie within the process itself. To me, that unpredictability was exciting, if also a bit risky insofar as it could literally make or break a business— its profits, its standing, its long-term relationships. In my experience, that's not just true of business but also of life.

I'll give you one example.

Nielsen wanted to purchase control of a Mexican media measurement company owned by IBOPE, which was itself owned by the Montenegro family in Brazil. IBOPE and Nielsen already had a joint venture in online media measurement, so the first step in our process was for Dave and me to fly to Brazil to meet with the brothers who ran the company and discuss how we might enhance doing business together.

For the first half hour of our meeting, the brothers gave us hell. According to them, we weren't supporting the venture well enough, and we weren't doing any number of things that they either needed or wanted. I was startled by the fact that before spending any time getting to know *us*, they simply launched into a litany of complaints. If there was any chance of our two companies moving forward together, we needed a do-over.

"I don't know how it is in Brazil," I said during a rare pause, "but I come from Israel, and when a guest makes a special trip from overseas to see you—and here, the CEO of Nielsen has come to see you—there would be a warm welcome. I was expecting to be welcomed, to engage in some small talk, perhaps share some coffee or a nice snack. Hospitality in Brazil is not what I expected."

From that moment, the whole meeting turned around. The change was so dramatic that it was almost hilarious to witness. They became the nicest people, willing to engage in productive conversation, willing to do business. They took us to lunch, then to visit their offices, and then we had a lovely discussion.

When we were all finally communicating at eye level, so to speak, it seemed to me a good time to propose something that Dave and I hadn't discussed ahead of time—an outright merger between our companies: "Why don't we join your company with our company? We will let you manage all of Latin America for us, and you'll make a lot of money by doing so."

One of the brothers jumped at the deal, and the other one asked for time to think about it.

I hadn't coordinated with Dave before proposing the merger. I simply went in that direction because the deal made good sense and the timing just seemed right. But that meant it was Dave who had to backtrack, reminding us all that any deal would need to be run past the lawyers, the board, and so on.

The thing about Dave—and our specific relationship—is that he didn't see my taking that opportunity to propose a merger as overstepping my bounds in any way. In fact, he seemed to appreciate that I was reading our audience and going with the flow of the interaction. Most CEOs would not have that same reaction.

But that's not what lies at the heart of this particular story.

A couple of months later, we finally approached IBOPE with the offer to buy control of the Mexican media measurement company they owned, which had been the goal of our visit in the first place. We negotiated a deal, and the only thing we had left to do was sign the papers. Elias, the guy negotiating from the other side, was a very proud Palestinian who was also Chilean. He owned a soccer team in Chile by the name of Palestine. On the backs of the team's jerseys was a version of a map of the Middle East in which Israel no longer existed.

Elias and I hit it off, and I'd gotten to know his personality during the process of hashing out the terms of the deal. When we got into the room to sign the papers, there were easily thirty people there—lawyers, accountants, all the people who make deals take clear and concrete form. Elias crossed the room and pulled me and our lawyer aside: "Listen," he began, looking concerned, "I miscalculated. The way the deal was structured, I am exposed, and I am going to have to pay taxes that I didn't count on, as much as twenty thousand dollars. I would like Nielsen to cover the tax."

"That is really not our problem," I said, "but let me talk with my team about it." I pulled my team out of the room and proposed that we cover the tax. What he was asking for wasn't much as far as Neilsen was concerned, and Elias was going to continue working with us as a board member. It made good sense simply to grant his request. Everybody agreed.

When we reentered the room, Elias was sitting far from the door. So, I raised my voice: "Elias, please come over here. We decided to give you what you requested."

From across the room, he shouted, "Thank you, thank you, thank you!"

Knowing Elias, his need for us to help him out, our need for him to become a cooperative member of our board, the quality of the relationship we'd developed over the preceding months, and the fact that he and I didn't see eye to eye politically, I announced, "There is one condition attached."

"Of course. Anything you want, anything you want."

"I want Jerusalem."

There was an abrupt and unique stillness in the room.

"Itzhak," he said with a shrug, "that's a little bit too much to ask."

Getting to know the person with whom you're negotiating is, at its heart, about establishing enough trust between you that you can recognize just how far you can push one another during the process. My joke could have blown up the deal. But both Elias and I knew that it wouldn't.

If really getting to know the people with whom you're negotiating is the first principle of negotiation, it might be fair to say that another is recognizing the importance of following up face to face in order to make progress. Let me give you just one example of the value of personal encounters in deal making.

Nielsen's primary competitor for syndicated reports—reports that present general market data and are sold to the industry—was the Middle East Market Research Bureau (MEMRB), an operation with a presence in twenty-six countries worldwide. MEMRB had $60 million in revenue and was losing money, so we had the idea of buying them out and thereby becoming the only game in town issuing these reports. For five years, my colleagues at Nielsen would come back from meetings with MEMRB's owner, who happened to also be the ex-president of Cyprus, saying that they couldn't come to an agreement with him.

I flew to meet this man and get a better sense for what was holding up the deal with Nielsen. At dinner, he and I discussed regional politics and got to know one another better. By the time we got to dessert, I felt comfortable asking, "So, are you going to sell us your company?"

"Of course I will sell, but nobody has given me an offer."

"But you have been talking to Nielsen for over five years now."

"Yes, and every time, some very nice person comes to talk with me, but no one ever explicitly makes an offer."

"Okay. Instead of negotiating, I'm going to give you an offer, and that's the offer, period."

"All right."

We left dinner having agreed to a deal. That was a relatively straightforward transaction, but I sensed it wouldn't have happened had I not connected with the company's owner to bring it about.

To this day, a lot of my friends ask me for negotiation advice, and the best advice I believe I can give them is this: develop the ability to negotiate in real time. Doing that depends on two things: establishing an in-person relationship and ensuring that the person you are negotiating with is also the person who has the authority to make decisions about the deal.

I tell my friends, if you are not 100 percent sure that you can negotiate a great deal in real time, listen carefully and then tell the other party that you need to get the proposed arrangement in writing so you can think about it. That said, whenever somebody I negotiated with used that strategy with me—asking for something on paper and time to think—it would drive me crazy! But that's mostly because I wouldn't get to bring into play my skill set for negotiating in the moment; our interaction would come to an end without a clear result. I suppose that's why I try hard to avoid negotiating with people who don't have the authority to make concessions right on the spot. So much more gets done that way! If the art of negotiating is reading other people to the point where you know they'll take the deal, you simply can't do that with someone who isn't authorized to do so.

When I see that I'm negotiating with someone who does not have the authority to decide, I won't disclose much. I might speak generally about what we're trying to do, but then I will always attempt to arrange a meeting directly with the decision-maker. Either that, or I'll send someone from my own team who is of equal position to the person sent by the other company. If there's pushback, I'll make my point explicitly: "I'm going to send one of my people to negotiate with you. The reason is that right now, you are negotiating with someone who *can* make decisions, but you don't have that authority. That puts my company in a bad position. If that's how you want to handle it, you will have to negotiate with someone other than me."

There are other subtleties of negotiation that I picked up along the way. Let's say, for example, that you work in an organization that gives you the authority to negotiate, but then you have to present the deals you've negotiated to the CEO and the board of directors. I've noticed that in those circumstances, with board members in particular, people may raise issues regarding details of the deal: "I don't really like this point, and I'd like you to change it …" What they don't understand is that the whole package you're bringing to them is essentially a done deal. Any detail that someone requests to change will reopen the whole deal for renegotiation. Whenever that would happen to me, I did everything I could to talk the person out of requesting a change.

No matter the specific details of any deal, I will always, always recommend doing one's homework prior to any negotiation about the people doing the dealing. It's ultimately how you find out what you have in common with someone. Not until you really get to know the person in front of you do you establish the trust you'll need to work together. I've walked into rooms where the person with whom I'm meeting knows everything about me. As a result, our very first conversation could go deep into our shared experiences rather than simply touch the surface of our commonalities and differences.

And in the end, if I don't connect with someone, I don't connect. There are many other people and many other deals to be made.

CHAPTER 23

Sometimes I think back to those psychological tests on which as a teenager I scored so highly that I managed to earn entrance into college when otherwise I might not have qualified. I ended up transforming those instincts into a genuine skill that's helped me be successful in business.

I think Ruthie may have always had a similar skill. She's good at reading people, and she's established working relationships with nearly everyone she encounters in our business dealings. She even regularly visits with the people at our local bank branch and the managers of properties we own. In fact, she's got a long-standing relationship with our accountant, Andy, not unlike the brief relationship she had with the artist who painted our portrait—at every meeting, she jokes that she conducts a bit of a therapy session with him, talking about family and personal matters right alongside any business concerns.

And we both still think fondly of the jobs I've held where a strong family-like environment existed within the workplace. We were lucky in those instances to find a balance between our personal and professional lives. We have good friends from across my career; we still go on vacations with some of the people I worked with at Aurec, and I still talk every handful of days with my friend Rami Belinkov, who was

VP of economics and logistics at Bezeq. I am proud of the reach and quality of the network I've established over the years, and I'm equally proud that I've been able to keep the number of people who might want to pick a fight with me to its barest minimum.

But no matter how much work one puts into establishing and maintaining relationships, there will always be people we do not hit it off with or situations where deals fall flat.

I've said already that negotiating with colleagues in Japan felt different to me, as aspects of their professional habits and their culture made it challenging to relate on a more personal level. I still clearly remember one situation that almost pushed me over the edge. One of Nielsen's big competitors was a publicly held company in Japan. Our company lawyer and I went for a meeting with the Japanese company's CEO, hoping to make an offer to buy them out. Our teams had arranged everything according to protocol and anticipated a format that we'd agreed upon ahead of time: I would present Nielsen to them, and then the CEO of the other company would present that company to us. But when I completed my presentation, the other company's CEO launched into a rant—all of it communicated through a translator: "I hate Nielsen. Your product sucks …"

After a handful of minutes, the translator stopped doing his job. The CEO ranted on, and the longer he did, the more ready to explode I felt. But our lawyer squeezed my knee under the table to remind me to control myself.

When the rant finished, I said to the CEO, "We should still try to do business together," handed over the chocolates we'd brought with us, and left the room. Once in the hallway, I asked the translator for more detail about what had been said. The translator replied, "He said such horrible things that you would not want to know."

Months later, when things were not going so well for this company, I scheduled another meeting with the CEO. This time, I attended it alone. After a brief and polite conversation, the CEO asked me directly, "Why did you come again?"

"You know, I'm Israeli; you're Japanese. But you seem to be more Israeli than Japanese. You are very direct, and I am going to be very direct with you. You're managing a company that is totally undervalued on the Japanese stock exchange. We came with open arms the last time we were here, and that is still the case now. We will make you head of our Asia-Pacific operation. You can make us better, and we can make you better."

I offered him $300 million, which was double the Japanese company's market value at the time. This time around, the response was a bit warmer. The CEO insisted that our two companies should be friends first and work on products together before considering a merger.

I felt as if some progress had been made. I don't think many other people would have returned to attempt another negotiation after such a hostile reception at that initial meeting. But I was unyielding. And at the end of the day, my Japanese colleague and I were communicating well, in stark contrast to the way our relationship began. I'd made progress that I hoped would lead, ultimately, to a buyout. But I never got to witness the outcome of that initial partnership or work on building a strong enough relationship. Within months of that visit and just after we had set in motion the product partnership my Japanese colleague and I had discussed in person, Dave left Nielsen.

I'd survived at Nielsen because Dave gave me as much rope as I wanted, and I managed not to hang myself with it. Without Dave as CEO, I was no longer interested in working there.

Before Dave left, he asked me to stay on for six months after his departure to help stabilize projects during the transition between

CEOs. That next CEO was Mitch Barnes, the same guy who had headed operations in China and who'd nearly lost his mind back when I said I wouldn't throw a table tennis game. Dave had followed the tradition of naming a successor years before he departed the company; managing Nielsen's operations in China was part of Mitch's preparation to take up the reins. I knew I could not work for him in the same way that I'd worked for Dave. That year alone, Dave's rope had extended long enough for me to establish seventeen separate joint ventures and strategic partnerships.

I agreed to stay for six months.

And that's how it came to pass that I solidified my belief that I could not work for Mitch.

A few years earlier, I had negotiated a five-year arrangement for Nielsen to pay the world's largest advertising and PR group, called WPP, $10 million a year for its top data boxes in US cable television markets. Everyone at Nielsen was happy with the deal because they'd expected we would have to pay much more than $50 million for that information. But after three years, we hadn't done anything with all that data. Dave left, and Mitch took his place. It was 2014, and I was in my final six months of employment at Nielsen.

Mitch asked me to negotiate us out of the remaining two years of the deal with WPP, so I called the CEO of Kantar Group, which was the research arm of WPP, and told him we wanted to renegotiate and that I understood we would need to pay them some compensation. We owed them $20 million for the two years that remained on the original contract. Kantar's CEO arranged to visit New York City with his team, and in preparation, I got my team ready for the negotiation. My assumption was that we might end up offering them $10 million.

Then, the day before the meeting, Mitch called me to say, "You are not allowed to negotiate for more than five million."

"Mitch, I know they will not take the deal for five million. They are coming all the way from London to meet with us. Everybody on that team bought a ticket. You're going to infuriate them, and they are our partner."

"I don't care. You're not authorized to do more than five million."

That was the end of the call.

I decided that if I had to tell them we were only offering $5 million, I was not going into that negotiation meeting without saying as much ahead of time. Again, I called Kantar's CEO, this time to let him know that my marching orders were the $5 million.

He had a fit. Three members of his team had already arrived in New York for the negotiation. The CEO was ready to fly out the next morning. "What kind of behavior is this?" he asked. "I thought we were negotiating!"

He hung up before I could answer.

The next day, Mitch received a call from Sir Martin Sorrell, the founder of WPP: "Take note: All the advertising agencies I know will stop doing business with Nielsen, and I'm going to say all the worst things about Nielsen in all its different markets. How dare you send this fucking Israeli to insult us by offering us only $5 million? Who the hell does this Israeli think he is?"

Mitch threw me under the bus. "I'm very sorry," he began.

And then he gave Kantar $20 million.

A year later, when I was no longer working at Nielsen, I attended a meeting with the global investment firm KKR to discuss with Sorrell a deal to buy a company in which Sorrell owned 20 percent. Mind you, he and I had never met in person. I introduced myself, and Sorrell went crazy at the mention of my name—I mean, he lost it. He was so furious, there was no deal.

When we left the meeting, the senior partner in KKR's New York office turned to me and said, "Never in my life have I gone to a meeting where Martin Sorrell was foaming at the mouth. He was going crazy at you. I'm amazed that you took it!"

"I just wanted him to calm down."

"You must have done something right representing KKR!"

That wasn't true, but I, too, had been impressed by Sorrell's outburst. I knew I had been the messenger of information that made him angry. But I hadn't imagined he could have such strong feelings about me, especially given that the two of us had never actually had a conversation with one another. The way I see it, his response speaks directly to my point about needing to establish a relationship when you're engaged in deal making. If you have a relationship and you have the leeway to negotiate, you have a much better chance of getting the best deal. If somebody else is pulling the strings, not so much.

Dave had left Nielsen, but before he did, he gave me a present. He arranged for Nielsen to put $10 million in an investment fund that I would start and manage. He knew that was one way I could keep bringing value to Nielsen, even if I wasn't working there anymore.

There was a stipulation in the fund's setup indicating that I would have to raise a minimum specified amount of money within the first year. I wanted to start working in the fund as soon as possible, so I asked Nielsen to invest its $10 million before I raised the rest of the fund's resources. That request needed approval by the board.

I asked Mitch to present my request at the next board meeting. The meeting took place, but afterward, I didn't hear from Mitch for several weeks. No one said anything to me about the change I had proposed.

I tried to schedule a meeting with Mitch, but according to his secretary, none were available. So, I sent Mitch an email inquiry.

He responded, "As you might have heard, the $10 million for the fund was approved by the board, but there was a discussion about you managing the fund while continuing in your current position for six months. The board decided that you cannot stay at Nielsen in your current position."

I was shocked. Had they decided to let me go? Without even telling me?

I tried again to schedule a meeting, and this time I was successful. When I walked into the room, I noticed that Mitch was actually shaking. So, I spoke right away: "Mitch, I totally understand where you are coming from. I'm fine with this. You have nothing to worry about."

He got up from his chair and gave me a hug with two kisses—one on each cheek.

Then he told me that there was one board member who didn't like me. That guy had stood up at the meeting and said to the group, "This is what I want." And he got it. Mitch hadn't offered a counterargument, but when the meeting ended, he turned to the company's lawyer and said, "This is not what I expected or what should have happened."

As we were finishing our conversation, I asked Mitch, "With whom do I negotiate my compensation before my departure?"

He offered me two options: the head of HR or the company's lawyer, who was also my friend. I chose to negotiate with my friend.

I started that conversation by pointing out what I took to be obvious: "You know that I have two years' compensation when I leave."

"Mitch didn't tell you?"

"Tell me what?"

"When the board decided to give you the fund, the same guy who proposed that you couldn't both run the fund and continue in your position also proposed that you not receive your compensation."

"I see." I could feel my anger rising. "You know what? I don't want the fund. I want my compensation."

"No, no, no. We are here to negotiate."

"Okay, let's negotiate." I thought for a moment. "I want a consulting agreement for two years at the compensation that I should have received."

"Done."

"And I want shares in the incubator program that I started for Nielsen."

"You'll have to pay what we paid."

"Fine."

To everything I asked for, my friend said yes.

We reached a point in the conversation where I couldn't think of anything else to request. We wrapped up the negotiation, and I stood up to leave the room. When I got to the door, I turned to my friend and said, "I want my phone to be paid for by Nielsen for two years."

He chuckled. "Are you serious?"

"Yeah. I'm very serious. No phone, no deal!"

"Itzhak, you have the phone."

The phone was nothing, a silly addition to a laundry list of things that actually mattered. But I couldn't have been more serious about leaving there with every possible benefit I could get.

CHAPTER 24

The incubator program in Israel was Nielsen's primary effort when it came to innovation. But the innovation aspect of that program dropped off in its later stages, when sustaining the selected projects and proving profitability became the primary concerns. So, when Dave decided it would be a great idea for me to manage a private equity fund with Nielsen as an anchor investor, he imagined that fund helping to fill out the company's innovation-centric function.

I found two partners—one of whom, Ziv Ben-Barouch, is still with me today.

Raising money for the fund was interesting. We had the $10 million investment from Nielsen, but we needed to close at least $30–35 million to start. I got the Tata Group, a giant Indian multinational conglomerate, to invest on the heels of Nielsen, and then we shifted to wooing private individuals. Some responded quickly to my pitch, each agreeing to a $5 million investment and signing off on the paperwork. Others took more convincing.

I twice pitched Ronald, and though he seemed amenable, he never signed the paperwork. So, I gave up asking, and in fact, I haven't met with him since. Around that same time, he'd started dating an

Israeli woman who seemed intent on disconnecting him from all his prior relationships with Israelis. I think she may have been quite successful overall. It's been almost a decade since the last time Ronald and I communicated directly, but our friendship with Fred Langhammer keeps us connected. Fred talks with each of us regularly and updates one about the other. I've said that even if I don't talk to Ronald for years, I will always remember that he gave me the opportunity to come to the US, which started me down a path that changed Ruthie's and my life. If he were to call me tomorrow needing my help with anything at all, I would show up for him in a heartbeat.

The funny thing about being a first-time manager of an investment fund is that I was once again in the position of having to learn on the job. And if there was one thing I was sure of, it was that I would invest in companies whose management teams had experience, even if that experience amounted to failure within the start-up environment. In hindsight, I can say that there were many things our inexperienced team at RSL did correctly simply because we followed our guts and because our guts (and our lawyers and all the talented people working for us) happened to be good enough guides. But now, when I sit across from the CEO of a start-up and start asking questions, if that person has run a start-up before, they inevitably offer me much more specific, much more professional answers. If an inexperienced person came to me with a great idea, I might still invest, but overall, I'm convinced that more experience is worth it.

I learned a couple of other things, too. First, I witnessed the fluctuation of valuations. Today, nobody pays whatever the valuation is. It's absolutely a buyers' market. Our fund had a big advantage investing in companies we could help design before setting them on their own courses. I see a lot of other funds where the investors come into an established company and want to tell those companies what to do. That is *not* what we did, and I think that's been a wise decision on our part. Honestly, I prefer investing in the very early stages of a company's formulation, because then I can brainstorm with them about the product, help them raise money, utilize my relationships to assist in getting them that first client or two, and so on. I enjoy actually offering and following through on the promises that lots of investment funds often only *say* they will do. I like being a strategic partner, rolling up my sleeves and working side by side with the companies in which we invest. I think that if you're an investor and you're not in the trenches with the company's management team, you are bound to have trouble understanding the issues they are facing. I've been where they are; I know the challenges that new companies face. Why wouldn't I offer to help them navigate territory that I've traveled, give them guidance I wish I'd had?

Second, I learned that managing a fund is a serious commitment of seven to ten years, maybe even longer. There's a general assumption that with a fund, you simply put money into companies for seven or eight years, then you sell those companies, and then everybody gets their money and maybe some profit. I, too, initially imagined that the time commitment would be up front—raising funds and selecting projects in which to invest. But here we are in year nine, and we still have five different active companies. Ziv and I are still responsible for the fund's limited partners, and at the time of this writing, our management fees will run out in about six months. We decided we will continue on regardless and strategize about what to do with the remaining companies. We made a commitment to these companies and to the investors, and we are going to see it through.

So far in the life of the fund, we've made fifteen investments, had seven successful exits, and have written off three companies. The remaining active companies have good valuations, which means our investors have an even bigger upside. And though not all the companies in the fund offer products or services related to Nielsen's interests, some of them made nice partners for Nielsen.

When I turn my attention away from the fund and look at all the different investments, over one hundred of them now, that Ruthie and I have made since the early 2000s, I can say that despite all the effort we put into research, interviewing, and due diligence, some of the best ideas can run into all kinds of issues—from technical dilemmas to sales difficulties—and struggle to survive. I'd say that over time we've grown savvier about our investments, but luckily those few companies that have been tremendously successful made up for all those that either did just all right or simply flopped. The nice thing for us now is that our investment history has paid off; today, it seems, great opportunities just come our way. Recently, one of my colleagues from RSL invited me to join him in lending money to a company that monitors residents' vitals in their nursing home rooms. Today, Medicare is their customer, and that company is about to sell on a $300 million valuation.

It's my opinion that assessing risk can be a tricky business. The person or company asking for money needs money, and getting that money can become their sole focus. But it's imperative for an investor to hold a broader view. That's why I take so seriously the part of investment negotiations that involves reading people and why I take into account everything I know about an investment opportunity before getting involved. Ruthie and I are not playing around.

CHAPTER 25

ack in December of 2013, we took a family vacation to
Australia with Gidi and Nina, Chooby, my nephew Yoni,
and his wife, Nili. Gidi and Nina had wed the year prior,
in 2012, at the New York Public Library. Having Nina
join our family was a great good fortune; she's smart and talented,
charming and steady. The wedding event was a joyous gathering of
family and friends with guests from near and far. We were able to
honor my cousin Gidon, my uncle Eliezer's boy and Gidi's namesake,
with both his sisters present.

I've said that Chooby and I share many traits, and one of those
is that neither one of us likes wasting time. What tops both our
lists of time-wasting activities is waiting in lines. I will always do
whatever I can to avoid a line. On the eve of the year 2014, on that
memorable Australian trip, when we all went to Sydney Harbour to
see the fireworks display, I didn't know people would be there who
had arrived at seven in the morning just to find the best spot from
which to watch. We Fishers? We left our hotel at eleven fifteen in the
evening for a show that started at midnight.

The roads and entrances all had police blockades, so I led the way
through the lobbies of buildings, the kitchens of restaurants, right

up to the harbor gate. The man at the gate looked at us as if we were insane to arrive so late.

"Do you have tickets?" he inquired, eyebrows raised.

I didn't know that we needed tickets. "We came all the way from New York to see these fireworks, and now you're going to stop us here because of the tickets?"

When he opened the gate and said, "Go ahead," I could see Chooby's eyes light up. Even today, he will do whatever he needs to skip a line—anywhere, even when he and his friends are just trying to get into a club—and he either gets let in or gets arrested.

Needless to say, even as an adult, Chooby has a way of focusing and keeping our attention.

By now, you know how much I enjoy traveling and having new and memorable experiences. Well, in 2016, to celebrate my sixtieth birthday, Ruthie and I, along with Jeff and Vivien, went on safari in a handful of countries in Southeast Africa. We started out in Tanzania, then visited Botswana, followed by Rwanda, and then finally Zambia. We came away from our time in Tanzania and Botswana with the same general impression: even in places that were very nice or clearly designed to offer tourists a good experience, there was still an element of the absolutely chaotic—everywhere seemed to be dirty, crowded, and loud. We arrived, exhausted, in Kigali, the capital of Rwanda, late at night. Before we disembarked the plane, the captain instructed us to leave behind any plastic bags in our possession. Rwanda did not allow them.

I dozed on the drive to the hotel, but Ruthie was wide awake and riveted by what she saw through the car window: the roads and sidewalks were spotless; everything seemed in perfect order. She woke me up to ensure that I witnessed it along with her. "Itzick, this place is very different."

She was right.

In Rwanda, nobody drinks or smokes in the streets. The country is spotlessly clean. One day every month, everyone, including the country's president, goes out and cleans common spaces. The children all go to school looking neat in their uniforms.

"You need to do something here."

You'll recall that those were Ruthie's words to me within the first twenty-four hours of our stay in the country. Now, whenever she complains that I travel there a lot, I remind her, "But you told me to!"

She replies, "I never knew that you would take it so far!"

After we returned home from the safari, I got to work making connections. Through a friend, I connected with Warren Buffett's son Howard, who is a member of the honorary council to the president of Rwanda and has been active in Rwanda through his nonprofit fund for the past twenty-five years. That connection made it possible to schedule a fifteen-minute meeting with Rwanda's president, Paul Kagame, during one of his visits to the United Nations in New York. He and I ended up talking for a full two hours, and during that conversation I expressed my interest in helping encourage foreign investments. The president invited me to visit Rwanda again, this time as his guest, and granted me access to the heads of government agencies. That welcoming gesture gave me a rush and was just the sort of thing I had enjoyed doing for colleagues and friends in Israel. I sensed that if all my efforts were met with such openness, without time-wasting bureaucratic stumbling blocks and barriers, I could make a real difference.

I'd done my research before making that trip and understood that plenty of people visit Rwanda, fall in love with the place, and immediately express interest in helping the country. But many either don't pursue that interest any further than its expression or support

THE COURAGE TO CONTINUE

a project or two, to minimal effect. Kagame himself had noted this publicly, pointing out to large audiences of foreigners, "All of you are very impressed by what you see here. What we ask from you is please, when you go, spread the word. Remember us and come back. Do not make this your only trip."

At the end of my visit, I met again with Kagame and let him know that I would not be one of those visitors to the country who displayed waning interest: "I'm going to start bringing people to make investments in areas that I think are important to the country, and I'm going to visit every three months." I knew that if I didn't follow up in person, with face-to-face meetings, no progress would be made, especially when I was promising to deliver results in a country where I do not live and cannot travel to easily. Without being present regularly, it would be as if I'd never been there at all.

The man who drove me to the airport after the meeting greeted me at the car, saying, "Thank you for helping our country."

I hadn't even gotten started, but his words of appreciation made me feel fantastic.

I've said that I see the parallels between Rwanda and Israel in terms of their histories of genocide and the fact that they're both very small countries, surrounded by enemies, and whose armies are known to be more powerful than their neighbors'. But what strikes me as remarkably *different* about the two places is that, whereas in Israel I often sense a general mood of paranoia at the heart of every business interaction, in Rwanda I've mostly experienced trust and openness. For example, in the past decade, Ruthie and I did a tremendous amount of work raising funds in the US for a university in the West Bank that educates Israelis and Palestinians side by side. It's true that we experienced the reward of raising an incredible amount of money for a great cause, but we also ended up quitting the task;

even though we paid all our expenses from our own pockets, the contractually agreed-upon 10 percent overhead for US operations and employee costs appeared to our Israeli partners as a form of stealing. I suspect these differences come down to how each country has dealt with what happened in its past and how each has decided to move forward. Israel has always seemed to me still raw, still nursing an open wound. In Rwanda, there is hope.

That said, my foray into encouraging business investments in Rwanda wasn't without its stumbling blocks. At my very first three-month visit, I brought with me a deal with a company that puts clips on electrical wires so that when a power outage occurs, the exact location of that outage can easily be determined. I was eager to arrange other deals—fertilizer-powered generators, shipping route cost optimization—but I failed miserably.

The reasons?

First of all, there was some disbelief about the seriousness of my commitment to help. When I arrived for that first three-month check-in, I heard someone say, "Hey, look! He's here again!" So many people didn't ever come back that they were truly surprised to see me. Second, as most everywhere else in the world, political and business maneuvering was happening behind the scenes. President Kagame made it possible for me to meet with whichever ministers I chose, but some of those officials already had their own well-established relationships with business interests and were not at all eager to have me bring other companies and investors onto the scene.

After my fourth visit, marking one full year of attempting to make deals for the country, my enthusiasm for doing good was close to being crushed. I met again with Kagame. "The most precious thing for me is my time," I began. "It is difficult for me to travel twenty-two hours to get here and then not be taken seriously. Please understand,

I want us to stay friends. I'm going to come once a year, because I already love you and I love this country. But I'm not going to continue on like this. It's just not working."

Kagame is a reflective, thoughtful, and precise man. He paused, said he was not surprised, and then he did something I found astonishing. He arranged for his cabinet to nominate me to become chair of the Rwanda Development Board, or RDB. All I knew about the RDB was that it had existed for many years and did not have a good reputation. But I trusted that Kagame had good enough reason for selecting this particular role for me, and I agreed to it.

By the time I was on my way to the airport from his office, I received a call from RDB's CEO. She was calling to inform me that I was being issued a diplomatic passport—a very helpful tool to have—on behalf of my new role in the Rwandan government. It seemed I was now being taken seriously.

CHAPTER 26

One of the many things that is unique about Rwanda is the number of women in positions of power. Women are CEOs, heads of banks; they constitute 60 percent of the members of parliament and 53 percent of the ministers. I've often suspected that the reason the country is so clean, so committed to the conservation of animals and to the recycling of plastics, and so up to date in its utilization of technology is that it has so many women in positions of power.

When I was appointed to the RDB, I was the only male board member. At its inception, the organization had been put in charge of all foreign investments, including exports, tourism, and a $300 million convention center considered the best in East Africa. Being chair of the RDB and holding quarterly meetings made a big difference in my overall efforts. Within another year's time, I felt like the machinery was up and running. I was able to breathe life into the RDB, I got to know all the parties that could help with our work, and I met with Kagame on each of my visits.

To increase my efficiency during the weeks that I visited, I asked Kagame for two permissions—to have a president's office license plate on my vehicle and to use Kagame's name during meetings with country officials when it felt like projects needed added momentum. The former would, quite literally, allow me to move through traffic with great ease, and the latter would convey to all parties involved in a negotiation that I had the president's blessing. It would make me, in other words, the person with decision-making power. Kagame agreed and added a third protocol: he instructed his cabinet that if a minister took issue with one of my projects, I would be given the opportunity to bring the project before the entire cabinet for discussion. I would present my case to the entire group, and the minister opposing me would be called on to explain the reason for whatever problem he or she had identified.

Those changes led to two significant results. First, I felt compelled to check in more regularly with Kagame to be certain that I could use his name in particular instances—it took some time for me to get used to having that broad permission from him. Second, from that point forward and to this day, no minister has raised an issue with my work that would necessitate us appearing before the cabinet.

One of my favorite things to do in Rwanda is solve bureaucratic slowdowns that impede bringing great new investments into the country. As I see it, by reducing red tape, I'm enabling projects to move forward that should have years ago as well as new ones that ought to move forward quickly once a deal is signed. I'll give you just one example of what I'm talking about. During one of my visits, I ran into a woman, Toni, who was about to leave the country after having tried for three full years to materialize her family's plan to invest $28 million into building a soccer academy that would include residential secular schools in five different regions of Rwanda. The family hadn't asked for typical incentives—tax write-offs, free land, and the like—and yet, in three years' time, no deal had been made. It was just my luck to have crossed paths with Toni in the lobby of the hotel where

I always stay. I was leaving for a meeting, and she was standing there, her bags packed, ready to leave for the airport. I heard her speaking in Hebrew and approached to introduce myself.

"You're not going anywhere," I stressed, after hearing her story. "Stay here one more day, and tomorrow, we will finish the agreement."

Toni didn't know me, and I'm near certain she thought I was crazy to make such a claim. But the next day, I gathered the ministers of education and sport, the country's lawyers, and Toni's lawyers for negotiations. Before the day was half over, we had reached a deal.

The more research I did, the more I learned about inefficiencies across the board. There were, for example, a lot of government-owned companies in Rwanda, which is admirable in the sense that the country is incubating new companies but also distressing because most of those companies were losing money. To see what I could learn about why most of the companies were operating at a loss, I gathered about fifty companies' CEOs into one room for a conversation. Watching them talk to one another reminded me of that early experience at the Nielsen off-site meeting when 250 people who'd never met were eagerly exchanging business cards.

To start the discussion, I asked an easy enough question: "Do your companies have a performance reward structure?"

Indeed, they did. Nearly all the companies followed the model of offering a thirteenth-month salary.

"Did any employee not receive the bonus salary this past year?"

Everyone shook their heads no.

That was at least one problem I could take care of quickly. Next, I asked the group to give examples of the challenges they faced in running their companies. The CEO of an aviation company talked about having no one on his board of directors with any knowledge of aviation. Another CEO said that he was his company's only employee.

By the end of the meeting, we had amassed an impressive list of impediments to business—just within these fifty companies alone. When I brought the list and my record of the meeting to Kagame, he decided on the spot to nominate a new minister to oversee all the government's companies. I was in the room when the new minister came for a meeting with the president. To start the meeting, Kagame pointed at me and said, "You should be thanking him for your job. I got so angry at what he discovered that I had to nominate a minister to fix it!"

As President Kagame expanded the reach of the RDB under my leadership to include areas like government employee education, I found myself taking on the unofficial role of chief negotiator for the country's biggest deals and operating in situations that had become problematic for the government. In one instance, after nine months of negotiations, a $100 million industrial park initiative remained stuck on two ridiculous details. The day after learning about this project, I got all the relevant parties into a room, told them they weren't leaving until they came to an agreement, and they signed a deal. In another instance, I negotiated on the country's behalf to improve a bad deal they had made with an Israeli defense supplier. The funny part of the story is that I came into the room and joined the Rwandan army's chief of staff, the minister of defense, and his deputies on one side of the table and then turned to our Israeli counterparts on the other side of the table and said, "You Israelis think we're stupid."

I registered the shock on their faces before listing off all their bad behaviors and then giving them one hour to come back with appropriate compensation. My Rwandan colleagues and I left the room. They hadn't expected me to take that approach, and they worried about the outcome. "Let's just give them a bit of time to think about it," I said, "and in the meanwhile, let's bet on what we think will happen." We all made our guesses about the amount of compensation the Israelis would offer—mine was the highest—and when the hour was through, the defense supplier came back to us with an offer that was much better than any of us anticipated.

Mind you, not every "problem" was that easy to resolve, and there were, and still are, times when I needed to call on Kagame to help push through a stuck deal—and not just by invoking his name.

In one instance, the government of Rwanda had decided to build medium- to high-income apartments in the capital city, Kigali. The apartments became a white elephant, standing empty for seven years, because the price of an apartment was only about $50,000 cheaper than the price of a house. I met with the head of social security and learned that the agency had $50 million in debt on its balance sheet from the apartments. So, I made him an offer: "Would you take $25 million to get the $50 million off your balance sheet?" The head of social security agreed, and then I told him that if he reduced the price of the apartments by 50 percent, they would be sold immediately. Six months went by, and he still hadn't made a decision one way or the other. In one of my conversations with President Kagame, he offered to take care of the deal for me. He put the heads of social security, the bank, and the CEO of the apartment project into a room and told them they were not getting out of that room until they agreed to my offer. They agreed, which was good, because we were able to lower the price of the apartments, sell all of them, and begin to build a phase two to add more.

One of the most difficult negotiations I've participated in was attempting to get the government out of a bad partnership with a gold mint factory. The government was a 50 percent shareholder but received zero revenue even though the factory was profitable and had a large turnover. My task was to get rid of the private partner. The partner complained that the Rwandan government was breaching its agreements and trying to push him out, so I had to dispel those complaints before pursuing the buyout. The negotiation was a lesson in preparation and in power. I did my research and ensured that we had all our ducks in a row, along with copies of all the paperwork the partner had signed. That meant I was able to meet each toothless complaint and unreasonable demand with actual signed receipts. It didn't help that the partner did the thing I dislike most—to three different negotiation meetings, he sent a lawyer in his place who did not have the authority to make decisions. That meant the partner was always in a position to receive concessions from us, but we would not be able to get anything from him. In the end, and nearly a year later, the partner himself participated in a meeting, and we were able to arrange for Rwanda to take control of the factory. The two outcomes of that negotiation? Rwanda got full control of the mint factory, and the Rwandan controlling shareholder started telling people that I negotiate "like a shark."

It took me some time to recognize that Rwandans will extend the negotiation process endlessly—even when there's hardly anything to negotiate about! Over the years, I've had to disabuse some of my colleagues of their seeming love for this activity. I suspect the primary issue is that no one wants to make the final decision. So, to help the people with whom I work closely, I tell them to use my name the same way the president allows me to use his—to get things done, and in a timely way. I've seen my colleagues become much more effective at their jobs and have even convinced many of them that it's better to make a decision and move forward than to hesitate or wait for someone else to decide. If, later, you discover that you've fucked up, fine; you acknowledge and take care of whatever happens when it happens.

The longer I've worked for the RDB, the more I've maximized the value of my time spent in the country as well as explored a host of different project areas. Today, we're moving forward with a project cultivating fish farming and another providing the infrastructure to feed every elementary school–aged child—all 1.5 million of them—an egg a day. Ruthie has taken over the egg project and is having fun overseeing its implementation. She's also done some consulting for start-ups about how to present themselves and seek funding.

I tell every potential investor across the globe that in whatever areas they work, Rwanda offers an opportunity to make a tremendous difference in people's lives.

There is a predictable—and ambivalent—response that I receive from some people, and it's one I enjoy dispelling. While people tell me they love Rwanda and the opportunities it offers, they sometimes comment on the country's policies, claiming it's a dictatorship, and cite human rights violations. To me, there is some genuine nonsense in those claims. I encourage people by saying, "Go to Congo, go to Kenya, go to Nigeria, and then we'll talk."

I make my case by sharing my personal experience witnessing President Kagame's commitment to Rwanda's citizens—especially when it comes to ensuring that the government is working toward greater equality. Often, this commitment of his comes down to the smallest gestures. When the COVID-19 vaccines were approved and being distributed globally, I learned that Kagame was not vaccinated. So, I immediately arranged for him to fly to a location where he could receive the vaccine. But Kagame put an end to that effort. He refused to be vaccinated unless all Rwandans had the same opportunity. Then, he helped Rwanda build a country-wide infrastructure to allow one of the major vaccine companies to install outposts that would refrigerate its product and help preserve its effectiveness.

A bit earlier, when the pandemic first appeared in the country, Kagame put very strict policies in place about safety and testing, including enforced curfews. For a time, everyone was required to be in their resting places for the night by five o'clock in the afternoon. Those who didn't obey this directive were picked up and transported to a local stadium for the night, where they were forced to listen to a loudspeaker recording issuing instructions about how to behave during the pandemic. Being me, I couldn't help but press Kagame during one of our conversations.

"Five o'clock is a little early for me, you know. What happens if I go out to eat, and they catch me?"

"You will be placed in the stadium, and you'll go through the process there!"

That response, and countless words and actions just like it, fits perfectly when I think about the massive transformational process the country has undertaken since the genocide of the mid-1990s. Kagame is always describing Rwandans as a polite and humble people. People who know who they are. People whose capacity to acknowledge and remember their past forms a foundation for hope, for unity, and for their commitment to lifting themselves into a better future.

As I see it, he was the one who made it so that they didn't have a choice but to continue living together in the same villages, working together in the same jobs. He set them on that path to reconciliation. Today, the economic situation is much improved, foreign investments are coming in, education quality is amazing, and the health system—which still has a way to go—is much better than it was. Compared to neighboring countries, Rwanda is like Switzerland or Singapore. Reconciliation may have been forced on its citizens in the beginning, but the results speak for themselves. It's taken a generation, but everyone is on the same page. They are one nation.

Not long before we were invited to name a baby mountain gorilla in Rwanda, we lost Ruthie's mother, Celia. She had a good and active life during the years she lived in the city, and she regularly spent time at our place. In all that while, she continued to be a perfect lady, agreeable, always measured in her comments, kind to everyone. I joke that she never said no to anything I suggested. Instead, if I proposed something that did not interest her, she would simply say, "We'll see," and leave it at that. Anyone overhearing her might think she was amenable to my suggestion, but those of us in her family knew that "We'll see" was the equivalent of "Nope, not happening." The one negative thing I ever heard her say was such a bold statement that I teased her about it endlessly afterward. In the midst of a conversation she was having with Ruthie, I overheard Celia say, "Well, of course!" Her tone was adamant. "Men are stupid!" She vigorously denied having spoken those words, no matter how many opportunities I took over the years to remind her of what she'd said. She would even call on Ruthie for support: "Ruthie, have I ever said that men are stupid?" Always the diplomat about such matters, Ruthie would answer, "Well, Ma, maybe once or twice."

After Celia died, Ruthie went to clean her apartment and, while going through piles of mail, discovered that she had contributed to nearly every Yeshiva in the state of New York. Celia and Leo both had left quite a legacy of giving—to their extended family and friends as well as to educational and cultural institutions. But when it came time to name the gorilla in honor of one of them, it was clear that Leo was the better choice. We imagined that after turning over in his grave, he might eventually enjoy knowing that he had a handsome round-faced namesake living in a sanctuary high in the Rwandan mountains. Both Ruthie and I found it difficult to imagine Celia feeling similarly, committed as she was, even in her final days, to modesty and decorum.

I mentioned that the year Ruthie and I participated in the baby-gorilla-naming ceremony, we brought a group of friends with us to the event, including pollster Frank Luntz, who had eaten schnitzel and played video games with Gidi during his stay in Israel in the early 1990s. Frank absolutely fell in love with Rwanda and now travels there on his own, teaching communications strategy at the African Leadership University in Kigali and bringing students to the US to visit government officials in DC or spend time training at places like Google headquarters in Mountain View, California.

Until that visit, Ruthie and I had avoided making any investments of our own in the country. As a government employee—but even before then, back when we first decided that I would do whatever I could, and at my own expense, to help encourage foreign investments—we wanted there to be no question that I was in Rwanda to work on behalf of the country and not in order to profit from any business deals. But during that 2022 visit, I wanted a couple of my friends to invest and help privatize the first government company, Gorilla's Coffee. To achieve that goal, I would also have to invest. I figured that of all the profitable projects I could possibly finance and all the fortunes I could make from doing so, no one would care about me putting a bit of money into a little coffee company.

My memory of this decision is that it was one of the few times I ever had a serious conflict with my wife. Ruthie reminded me of our initial agreement: no making money in Rwanda.

So, I made a deal that any money that came to us from the investment would stay in Rwanda for philanthropic projects. Still, she thought it was a bad idea. She took issue with the possibility of our making *any* money from *any* investment in Rwanda, quickly identifying potential negative effects it could have on all my other efforts.

So far, I have been safe from any repercussions, especially those involving Ruthie's wrath. But as I like to say, you never know.

CHAPTER 27

One of the achievements during this time of which I'm most proud is working with Rwanda's minister of youth to introduce a start-up competition. The year of the first big event, Ruthie and Chooby came along with me to get things rolling, and Chooby, with his start-up experience, worked directly with the inaugural team to structure the competition. In six months' time, we put together an excellent contest, televised on national TV, with the president and me awarding first-prize funding to the winning company. Since then, every twelve months we host another competition. Between the first and third competition cycles, applications rose from around a thousand to over five thousand, and the number of sophisticated technology companies vying for the prize increased dramatically. Each year the top ten companies are invited to participate in a Swedish incubator program to help them achieve commercial success.

When I started working for RDB in Rwanda, the most common complaint I heard from every minister was that so much time and money were being wasted; for all the country's apparent efforts, corresponding results were not evident. I'm proud of my contributions to turning that around. Last year alone, we generated $1.2 billion in foreign investments.

In fact, my effort has been recognized in ways I hadn't dared hope it would! This past year, I was promoted to chair the Rwanda Mining, Petroleum and Gas Board, or RMB. How did that happen? The president asked me to look into the situation with the country's minerals, because mining projects didn't seem to be moving.

"Looking into it" showed me that the industry was not working the way it should. The Rwandan government gave over 200 concessions to 132 companies for conducting exploratory mining. But a lot of these companies were letting artisans—private miners or pirates—do whatever they wanted. On top of that, workers faced significant safety issues, and a lot of cash leakage occurred within the industry overall because there were too many middlemen.

I reported my findings to the president, and he was livid: "This is not what Rwanda is about! This is not who we are!"

"My recommendation to you is this: I took on the RDB, and I think you are happy with where we are six years later. I suggest you find somebody who is going to do the same for the RMB."

Kagame answered, "But I have nobody like you."

"What does that mean?" I began.

"I would like you to do it. You are coming every three months anyway."

"How about I try it out for one year and see if I can be effective? If I cannot, then you find somebody else."

When I met with the mining board for the first time, they had not had a meeting in over a year. I explained our new, more frequent meeting schedule as well as how the board would operate going forward. From that conversation, I was escorted to a meeting of five hundred miners, where I was told I had to give a speech.

"How long?" I asked. "And on what am I speaking?"

I told the miners that the days of lawlessness were over. The government would start taking concessions away from companies that did not live up to the obligations of their licenses and contracts. The cash leakage—as I saw it, the product of not paying workers fair wages—would come to a halt. I would personally make sure that the industry thrived.

I didn't reveal it at that gathering, but I had already started negotiating an arrangement between the Rwandan government and the second-largest mining company in the world. That in itself is a big deal, given that Rwanda is not yet considered a mining country. Surveyors claim $179 billion in minerals is in the ground. I think that's an exaggerated claim. But if there is even 10 percent of that amount, it could change the entire country.

Today, I'm negotiating all mineral deals and licenses on behalf of the government. The woman who is helping me do all this work is now a full-time employee. So far, we've pulled about forty licenses from companies that were not at all fulfilling the terms they'd signed off on; other companies are being given the opportunity to get themselves in order and come back with an argument in favor of preserving their licenses. I am putting plans in place to address piracy and safety issues and generally bring the industry to order.

For all my hard work cleaning up policies and processes and ensuring that companies contracting with the government are living up to their agreements, it may turn out that the most notable thing I've achieved for the Rwandan people came about from a handful of well-timed phone calls.

Reed Hastings, board chair of Netflix and a friend of Frank Luntz's, told Frank that he wanted to accompany him on one of his Rwanda visits. Frank arranged for them to give a joint TED Talk in

Kigali, and I decided it was absolutely crucial for Reed to meet the president. There was no specific project for them to discuss, but my gut told me this was an important connection to make. The president was traveling abroad during the visit, but I insisted that he return to Kigali to dine with Reed, no matter what arrangements had to be made to get him there. Kagame flew in minutes before sitting down to dinner with Reed and then reboarded his plane and flew out again immediately afterward.

The result of that meal? Reed gave $50 million to provide smart-phones for 1.2 million homes at a rate of twenty dollars a month, including unlimited data usage. And since then, he's invested in agritech companies set to develop African products for local consumption.

You never know!

When it comes to that phrase, I suppose it's worth recognizing that not every encounter is a beneficial one. I've occasionally been surprised by the people who seek me out because of my involvement in Rwanda.

Not that long ago, I got a call from a sheik from the United Arab Emirates who proposed a project for electronic license plates that include toll road passes, easy payment for parking, and so on. It was a nice idea, though I'm not sure Rwanda would be the first country in the world I would choose to implement it. The sheik wanted to create a factory in Rwanda to manufacture the plates and then have the government purchase plates for every car in the country.

On top of that, he wanted to meet with the president.

Something felt off, so I decided to establish a boundary: "The president will not meet with anyone unless they are actually investing money in the country," I clarified.

"I don't think you understand me," he said. "Not only am I going to build the factory in Rwanda; you and I are going to sign a special deal."

Yikes.

The second he said that, any chance of a future deal was dead.

But for every suspect proposal, there is someone who makes something good happen. I took my dear friend Rami, from Bezeq, to help address a government liability of $132 million in Rwanda's telecom operations—the result of a bad deal the Rwandan government had made with a Korean telecom company. Rami sat in on a couple of meetings, got hold of the contracts and supporting documents, and gave everything a very thorough review. Since then, he's returned to the country on his own to help resolve the matter. To me, that's more evidence of the amazing speed with which people fall in love with the country and want to do good there.

My work in Rwanda is getting more gratifying rather than less. This past year, I took Gidi, our son-in-law Mikey, and Ruthie's cousin Jay for a five-hour climb in the forest to visit Leo and the other gorillas. They went to the market, dined in fancy galleries and restaurants, and participated in a meeting of the RDB and a discussion with government ministers about addressing demand for affordable housing. This year, I've suggested to Ruthie that when she and I visit for the twentieth-anniversary celebration of the mountain gorillas, we stay in the country for a full two weeks. "We'll see," is what she's so far said to me, but I hope that will lead to a more positive outcome than if her mother had spoken those words. I think we should spend some time there enjoying ourselves in addition to all the work we'll be doing.

The president sent us word that when he's next in New York City, he would like to spend time with the whole family. Ruthie says that if he wants her to cook the brisket that I've bragged about, he'll need to give her notice well ahead of time. She makes this request because Kagame once came by our apartment unanticipated. At two in the afternoon we learned that he would be stopping by at five. We both rushed home to be there when he arrived, and he stayed for five hours, enjoying some wine and intense conversation. He and I got carried away in our conversation, and poor Ruthie found herself starving. She finally left us and grabbed a snack from the kitchen, mortified that he'd stayed through dinner and she had nothing to offer him. She vowed that wouldn't happen again.

It's become clear to me that in Rwanda, with Kagame, I am repeating a version of the arrangement I had with Dave Calhoun at Nielsen. I have my rope to do with as I choose, as long as I do not hang myself. And as with Dave, if Paul Kagame leaves the presidency, I'm sure I'll leave as well.

I know that what takes generations to build can be destroyed in a remarkably short period of time. So, I will continue to value deeply every trip I make, every bit of effort I put toward the good of that country. And whenever someone there says to me upon arrival, "Welcome home" and "Thank you for helping our country," when I leave, that will still be worth more to me than any amount of money in the world.

CHAPTER 28

mentioned that my son-in-law, Mikey, Chooby's husband, came along on a recent trip to Rwanda, with Gidi and Ruthie's cousin Jay. Now he is unfortunately our ex-son in law. Mikey is amazing—seemed like a perfect partner for Chooby and another welcome addition to our family. Theirs was the very first gay wedding held at the Plaza Hotel, and it was a joyous celebration. At the rehearsal dinner, Ruthie and I pointed out that when we first met Mikey, we each came to the same conclusion: if Chooby wasn't going to date him seriously, we would. After all, he's bright and hardworking; he's dimpled, with jet-black hair and a beautiful face. Everyone wants to be around him, and he's even a great cook. What's not to adore?

Shortly after Chooby and Mikey got engaged, the three of us were together at a bagel shop in our neighborhood. The man taking our orders looked at Mikey, then at me, and asked, "Is this your son?" I corrected him, gesturing at Chooby, "No, *this* one is my son, and this is his friend."

I caught hell for not introducing Mikey as Chooby's fiancé.

I understood that Chooby—the guy who told our dentist before he confirmed to me and Ruthie that he was gay—would happily out himself to whomever he met, so when Ruthie and I took him to help with the start-up competition, I worried about how he would be received in Rwanda. I didn't know what Kagame's reaction would be, but when I indulged my compulsion to speak to him directly, he was totally open minded and welcoming.

I remember that when Chooby first came out to me and Ruthie, I felt like the sky was falling. Looking back on it now, I think how funny it is, what you can get used to with time. Not only were we able ultimately to adjust to Chooby's announcement; we've also never had an issue fully supporting his choices. Like I've said before, we are enormously lucky to have the family we do.

And we feel very sad that after all that Chooby and Mikey got divorced. But life goes on and we hope everyone will be continuing on a good path.

Both Chooby and Gidi continue to entertain their entrepreneurial inclinations. After leaving Nielsen and pursuing his own start-up, Gidi eventually chose a position at JetBlue Ventures, launching an innovation program with a $100 million venture capital fund focused on travel and hospitality. That venture invested in about twenty-five companies and ensured that the airline could utilize some of the technology it was helping develop. I think what Gidi liked most about that job was the way it removed the risk factor and made it easier to experiment with new technologies. He would pitch a project internally, run proof of concept, and then introduce a pilot program or short-term implementation to demonstrate overall value. Nina worked for Estée Lauder International, earned her MBA at Wharton, spent some time developing a start-up company for designers, and then headed up marketing for another start-up focused on creating activities for children, both on- and offline.

Nina is our daughter and we are so blessed to have her in our lives.

Gidi and Nina started a family of their own, bringing our three sweet grandchildren into the world. Ella, Lev, and Brody are the three best things that ever happened to us. Ella is a very smart, very adorable little woman. She loves school and being with friends. Lev is a super handsome dinosaur-loving little guy who also happens to have the Leo-Gidi thread running through him. He's only five years old, but he insists on walking Ruthie to the door to say goodbye and make sure she is okay. Brody is a sturdy, strong boy, lively and smiling at all times. Nina is an even-keeled and warm mother, and Gidi is fully engaged in his parenting duties. They do a wonderful job juggling all their responsibilities. It's such an immense pleasure to spend time with them and watch their children grow. They make us laugh and cry with joy.

It also makes Ruthie laugh that Gidi—the very same child of ours who, after going to Jewish schools all the way through the twelfth grade, declared that he was never going to talk to another Jewish person, let alone ever send a child of his own to Jewish school—joined a Jewish fraternity in college and now insists (insists!) that his own children have to attend Jewish day school, even if that means he has to drive them quite a distance to get them there.

Not long after I left Nielsen, Chooby decided he needed to earn an MBA. Initially, I wasn't supportive of the idea; my thinking was that nobody cares what degrees you have or where you got them, especially when you already have a strong network of connections. But Chooby did his thing and earned his degree from Cornell Tech. He joined forces with a couple of friends he met there, along with a friend from his Nielsen days, and together, the group developed a start-up project that sold a scheduling platform for service professionals like lawyers, doctors, and hairdressers that functioned entirely through text messaging rather than through a web scheduling system.

Today, Chooby is working on a new start-up venture, and he regularly calls me for advice about raising money and conducting negotiations. Gidi moved on from the venture arm of JetBlue to a huge German reinsurance company called Munich Re, where he ran an innovation lab that ideates and pitches start-ups. More recently, Gidi and I have been making some investments together. As his kids reach school age, he's rediscovering his appetite for getting out of a corporate environment and back into start-ups.

Over the years, Ruthie and I have expanded our investments in art to include the theater, which has been a tremendously edifying way to lose money. Ruthie has been on the board of an impactful theater company called the Tectonic Theater Project, I've been part of the International Emmy Awards board, and we've both held producer titles for some award-winning plays. This past year, Ruthie's investments won seven Tony Awards. We sent Chooby and Mikey to the awards ceremony with instructions, from me, to join the others up on stage if any of our plays won. When they did, he texted Ruthie from his seat, "Do I really have to go up on stage?" I laughed, thinking that, if it were me attending, I would have run up there with all the others, waving my hands in the air, an enthusiastic open-mouthed smile on my face.

Back when I was on the board of the International Emmys, there was an annual meeting in Israel, and I had the idea that it was important for Bibi to talk with the group. Needless to say, Bibi was undecided until the last minute about attending. In the end, he gave a nice presentation, and as the whole group was moving on to the next activity, he turned to me and said, "Itzhak, could you join me, please?" I followed him and his security team back to his office, where we sat and talked freely about any number of things. The army chief of staff came by for a scheduled meeting. The foreign minister came by for a scheduled meeting. Each time, Bibi instructed, "Let them wait."

When I left his office, his chief of staff pulled me aside: "This was a very important meeting."

"How so? We talked about this and that. Nothing significant."

"He doesn't have any friends he can talk to openly."

I thought back to all the meetings I'd sat in on as treasurer for Bibi's campaign and, afterward, for the Likud party. Back then, I'd been astounded by the horror politicians showed when they were forced to consider retiring from their roles or losing an election. I remembered, too, when Bibi lost the 1999 race for prime minister. Neither he nor Sarah could imagine their lives without position and power. Today, a lot of people approach me to say, "You helped invent this problem we are having," referring, of course, to the leader Bibi has become. I explain that he has undergone a dramatic transformation from those early years, that he is very different now from the person he once was. In many ways, he is the complete opposite, a paradox in human form.

Israel, too, seems very different to me today. Yes, it has always been an uneasy collection of people from all over the world, representing many different cultures and religious sects. And yes, it has always had internal issues and inequities in need of addressing. But those internal issues always conceded priority, lining up behind the country's need to defend itself against its enemies. I've often thought that Israel might be held together by that outward focus; if it ever achieved peace with its neighbors and turned its attention inward, perhaps it would fall apart.

And though we have always worried that our enemies would come into the country to slaughter us, before October 7, 2023, no attempt had ever left so many brutally injured and dead.

I was born in the middle of the 1956 war. I lived through 1967, 1973, two incursions in Lebanon, the war in Gaza, terrorist events, Gulf Wars I and II, missiles overhead, suicide bombers throwing themselves next to children, and all the rest. It's hard to say that one gets used to it, but having grown up in Israel, I expect that these things can happen. I know that if I am meant to die, I will die. If there is a bullet or a bomb or a missile with my name on it, there is nothing I can do to keep it from reaching me.

A couple of years ago, Ruthie and I were driving along the highway near Tel Aviv when we heard sirens. We looked up and saw the Iron Dome intercepting and exploding incoming rockets. We got ourselves back to our hotel, where many of the people around us seemed scared; others were completely hysterical.

The two of us were as cool as cucumbers. We both find hysteria unproductive. I have always been like this, and in our long life together, I have discovered that Ruthie is a lot like me in this way.

That said, what happened in October 2023 broke all the rules. As I later watched an interrogation of one of the captured terrorists, he was asked, "What was the purpose of this attack?"

"Kill, kill, and kill," he answered.

Here was an event that awoke all the traumas we inherited from our parents. I know our parents found what happened to them incomprehensible; today, I find myself relating to their experience a bit differently than I did before.

When the war with Hamas began, I thought the events of early October were more a blow to the Israeli psyche than an existential threat. But now, just a few months later, I see things differently, and in the back of my mind is a question about the disappearance of the state of Israel. When I was young, perhaps I should have been more worried about the exact same thing, but I trusted the country's leadership, its army, our spirit.

Today, Israel is on fire. The events of October 2023 proved that the defense technology we put in place was not good enough and that a neighboring country like Lebanon poses a threat against which the Iron Dome cannot protect us. Inside the country, and leading up to October, hundreds of thousands of Israelis demonstrated against the government's attempts to consolidate power. The state of Israel is supposed to be a safe place where Jews are not persecuted, where we are the majority in terms of language, culture, and religion. But we Israelis are right now not one people. Even the inside is not safe.

In the wars of my youth, the rest of the world looked at Israel as the underdog and cheered when we successfully defended ourselves. But in the time since, our reputation on the world stage has deteriorated. Now—or again?—the country is taken to be a perpetrator of unconscionable violence.

I think about our friend Vivien's mother, who went to live in Aruba after her husband died. She was in her seventies at the time. At one of her doctor visits, the conversation turned to the fact that she was Jewish.

"You're Jewish? I can't believe you're Jewish!" was the doctor's initial response. Vivien's mother had red hair and was native Spanish.

The doctor saw fit to add, "When are you going to give up talking about the Holocaust and making people feel guilty about it?"

Vivien's mother quipped back, "When are you going to give up blaming us for the killing of Christ? Who's held the grudge longer?"

*

CHAPTER 29

always say that Ruthie and I have a lot in common, even though we grew up worlds apart. But as we've grown older, a difference in our perspectives on life keeps bubbling to the surface.

I look to the future and say something like, "I have another twenty years to enjoy life and try new things."

In contrast, Ruthie looks back and says, "I had a great life."

You'll remember that Ruthie insisted we not write this book. When we started working on it, she asked questions like, "What on earth have we got to talk about?" And now that we're finishing the process, I hear her asking, "What is my life about?"

That is Ruthie's question; it's absolutely not mine. But when you live with Ruthie, you cannot avoid dealing with that question. If you forget, she reminds you.

She asks a very important question. How you answer it is also very important, because there's a way of answering that can quickly depress you to the core. When some people take time out from their daily lives to think about the bigger picture, if they don't see a clear aim or they don't target the things that make them feel motivated, they can really struggle when it comes to mental health. And I'm talking about people generally, not even those who have baggage similar to our own.

After the World War II, there were survivors who killed themselves. For many who were able to find ways of moving their lives forward, the concern with lineage, with the continuity and history that spans generations, became the primary focus. To have children and raise a family was to help ensure that the tree would not be cut down entirely, as the Nazis wanted. So, when Ruthie asked her father, "What does it all mean?" he would answer, firmly, "We keep going."

But we are the next generation.

Ruthie and I are on the same page about refusing to be obsessed with death. Death is going to come. There is nothing we can do about it. We both still believe that having children and grandchildren is incredibly important, and the highlight of our lives will always be our kids. As I say, we're truly crazy about them, insane for believing they can do no wrong. We also want to be close not only to our kids and grandkids but also to all eleven of our nieces and nephews and be directly involved with them as much as we can.

But we have questions, too, about our broader purpose beyond survival. Sure, when I was growing up, survival was at the front of my mind. I went into the armed forces believing that the most important thing I could do was stay alive. But as I've matured, I've developed a different mentality.

Staying alive and having children are no longer the *only* important things. Both Ruthie and I have arrived at a place where we wonder what more we can do to leave a positive mark on our families and the world.

When I look right and left, I see that there are always experiences we can have and lessons we can adopt from other people. But I tell Ruthie all the time, "We are blessed to be where we are." And I make sure also to remind her, "We have another twenty years to make some additional difference in the world, to make other people's lives better."

Ruthie says she used to laugh whenever she heard anyone talk about the importance of leaving the world a better place. It seemed like such a trite comment. But when you get older, you find yourself asking, very seriously, "How am I going to leave things for the ones who live after me?" And you see, that's not a depressing question—it's a great one!

I can tell that Ruthie thinks so, too. Because if I want to really get under her skin, I discuss retirement. Her friend's husband recently retired, and now he spends all his time going from one doctor's appointment to the next. This is exactly how Ruthie and I picture it: You have nothing else to do, so you start checking in with your doctors. And then you start finding all these issues in need of medical attention. That's the reason Leo and Celia never vacationed with their friends in Miami. Leo was afraid the friends were going to either spend all their time talking about their ailments or pull him directly into the grave.

"Go for a weekend," I would suggest. "You have a whole group of friends there!"

"No, no! We are not taking any chances on getting dragged in."

So that Ruthie wouldn't have to consider spending time in Miami, we looked for a house in the Hamptons. It took five years before she found one she liked that was big enough for the kids, their friends and families, and all our friends to gather. This past summer, even while shuttling back and forth to work in Manhattan, Ruthie entertained hundreds of people there.

When she looks back, Ruthie insists that my career was much bigger than hers, but I don't understand what she means. "What career?" I ask, well aware that whatever I've accomplished, there would have been no doing it without her direct assistance. Sure, we joke about how easily she agreed to all my nonsense, stopping one kind of work and starting another, indulging my entrepreneurial spirit, taking big risks along the way. But she was right there, working beside me. I ran around chasing deals with Ruthie running after me, papering them as quickly as she could. Whenever I am involved in a negotiation, Ruthie is behind the scenes, giving me her list of comments on all the details of the deal. Each time I start a negotiation process by saying, "My lawyer gave me these remarks," and direct us to focus on the list one by one, I know that Ruthie is driving the entire conversation.

For good measure, I'll sometimes add, "I sleep with my lawyer," just to see how many eyebrows are lifted, how much awkward laughter sputters up from the group.

If Leo were alive, I imagine he might say, "Look what she did with this Litvak!" Even our cousin—my very own blood relative— once ran into a friend of Ruthie's in a shopping center only to tell that friend, "Ruthie is a genius! Look at how she molded Itzhak!"

Our parents were persecuted for being Jewish. But after everything, they gave us the opportunity to extend the family tree, set a good economic base, and live good lives. And now we are giving our kids that opportunity—and other people as we are able—so that they and their kids can have full lives and realize their potential.

I imagine that the next generation will have a different answer to the question "What is my life about?" Although in 2023, they received a blunt reminder that people still hate and are trying to kill Jews.

Today, there are hate crimes and school shootings. Gidi called us recently to say that horrifying graffiti had been scrawled on the side of a grade school in their neighborhood. When our grandchildren are in my care, I am a nervous wreck about them. I want nothing more than to hold them tight.

What was it that Leo said to me when he welcomed me into the family? "Let it be. Let life be." It's a lesson I take seriously, though I've been surprised that it's gotten a bit harder rather than easier to follow the more our little family grows.

As if to echo Leo's sentiment, at every holiday gathering, we take our seats around the table and our cousin Jay offers his usual toast: "They tried to kill us. Let's eat!"

And then we have a lovely meal and go on with our lives, doing what we can to make them good ones.

EPILOGUE

M y grandfather lived for eighty-nine years. We have a few sheets of paper on which he wrote about his experience trying to protect his family from the Nazis. We cherish those pages, but they are thin documentation of one particularly harrowing period in the course of a life.

Working on this book, I felt it was important to account for what happened in our families before Ruthie and I came to be. Together, we talked about how to share with you some of what was brought into our lives by those who preceded us. Attempting that history, brief and inadequate as it appears in these pages, was also a way of acknowledging the weight we have always felt on our shoulders.

Hopefully, this book is less a weight than a window.

Windows always frame particular views. They offer those who look through them a unique perspective on a given scene. Occasionally, too, depending on the way the light refracts on the surface of the glass, a window can give those who look a quick glimpse of themselves, opening their eyes to the potential of different perspectives.

Two hundred years from now, when our descendants find this book, they will learn something about their family. What will they see? The shadowy contours of a handful of survivors? The sketch of a couple who couldn't ever have imagined the trajectory their lives would take?

At first glance, this story might seem like that of an ordinary kid who struggled in school and lacked clear career goals. But over time, that narrative evolved through the risks I took in business and life. More importantly, it led my wife and me to become part of a long chain of continuity, honoring both our families and our people. Over the years, we've traveled far—personally and professionally—building a track record of business success while striving to make a positive impact in the world.

Now, as parents and grandparents, we are deeply committed to family and the lessons handed down by our ancestors. I've learned that when you dedicate yourself to finding meaning in your life, anything is possible. You don't need to have it all figured out beforehand—life's path often reveals itself as you go.

Like I said at the start, if you find yourself reading this book, it's quite possible that we are your ancestors. That may mean you also have possession of a painting of the two of us, created in the year 2019. In our will, we passed that painting down to our sons, Gidon and Ron, with the following stipulation: access to the funds that make up their inheritance requires that this strange and haunting painting spend six months a year in each of their family homes for the remainder of their lives. Of course, we added one further detail: the painting cannot be housed just anywhere inside their residences; it must be hung on the wall directly opposite their beds, thereby ensuring that when they wake each morning and close their eyes each night, they get a good look at that very strange rendering of us.

You should know that they didn't find our joke at all funny.

Consider this book—strange, too, as it may seem—the companion piece to that painting. Actually, that's one of the ways I convinced Ruthie to let me write the thing—surely she wouldn't want that portrait to be the only depiction of our lives left behind for our descendants!

Looked at side by side, two artifacts among the many other things we have created and accumulated in this lifetime, maybe you'll see something more than Botox Guy and Bad News Lady, or Itzhak's deals and Ruthie's lawyering. Maybe you'll see two people deeply committed to honoring their humble beginnings and contributing to a future in which the redemption of individuals and of entire peoples is yet possible.

After all, anything is possible. You never know.

ABOUT THE AUTHOR

Over the past three decades, Itzhak Fisher has been an angel investor in eighty-five start-ups worldwide with an impressive IRR. In parallel, he deployed over $3 billion of investments and built new ventures during his tenure as EVP, M&A, and Global BD at Nielsen Holdings. He was the chief executive officer of RLS Communications and the chairman and cofounder of BuzzMetrics. He is a seasoned global executive with a passion for technological innovation and start-ups, which began when he first fell in love with computer science. His reputation in the entrepreneurial and investment world spans across the US and Israel.

Itzhak is a consultant to KKR and Goldman Sachs. He is a member of the NYU Courant Institute advisory board, the chair of the Rwanda Development Board, and a trustee at NYIT. Itzhak was born and raised in Israel but has lived in New York City for the past twenty-three years.

www.ingramcontent.com/pod-product-compliance
Lightning Source LLC
Jackson TN
JSHW021620090425
82320JS00007B/28